The Everyday Life of the Clans of the Scottish Highlands

Michael Newton

The Everyday Life of the Clans of the Scottish Highlands

Copyright © 2020 Michael Steven Newton

All rights reserved. Except for brief quotations, no part of this book may be reproduced in any form, or by any means, without permission from the author.

Published 2020 by Saorsa Media.

Paperback ISBN   978-0-9713858-2-5
eBook ISBN   978-0-9713858-3-2

Introduction — 1

Studying History, Using Sources — 5
What is History? What is Historical Research? — 5
Sources: Primary and Secondary — 7
Introduction to Gaelic Literary Tradition — 10
Reading Sources Critically — 15
- Authorship and Origin — 15
- Subjects, Content and Context — 15
- Genre — 15
- Agenda and Argument — 15
- Interpretations — 16
- Inter-relations Between Primary Sources — 16

Divide and Conquer — 17
Feudal Scotland — 17
Highlands and Lowlands — 20
Identity and Ethnicity — 23
Primary Sources — 26
- Unknown, Lebor Bretnach "The Book of Britain" — 26
- Unknown, Chronicles of the Scottish People — 28
- The Declaration of Arbroath — 28
- John Mair, The History of Greater Britain — 29
- George Buchanan, The History of Scotland — 30
- Thomas Morer, A Short Account of Scotland — 31
- William Buchanan, The Family of Buchanan — 32
- Edmund Burt, Letters from the North — 32
- Rev. John Macpherson, Critical Dissertations — 33
- Anne Grant, Essays on the Superstitions — 34

What's In A Name? — 36
Personal Names — 36
Kin-Groups and Terminologies — 40
Clan Reputations, Rivalries, and Nicknames — 43
Clans, Tartans and Badges — 47
What of Clan Septs? — 48
Primary Sources — 49
- Edmund Burt, *Letters from the North* — 49
- Alexander Nicolson, *Gaelic Proverbs* — 50
- Rev. John G. Campbell, *Clan Traditions and Popular Tales* — 52
- William MacKenzie, *The Book of Arran* — 53
- T. D. MacDonald, *Gaelic Proverbs* — 54
- Anonymous, "Clan Nick-Names" — 55

As Old As The Mist — 57
He Who Controls the Past… — 57
Primary Sources — 59
- *The Origin of the MacDonalds* — 59
- *The Origin of the MacKenzies* — 61
- *The Origin of the Macintyres* — 62
- *The Origin of the Campbells* — 63
- *The Origin of the MacRaes / MacRaths* — 65
- *The Origin of the Mackintoshes* — 65
- *The Origin of the Buchanans* — 67
- *The Origin of the Grants* — 68
- *The Origin of the MacLeans* — 69
- *How the MacDonalds Got Possession of Dalness* — 70
- *The Origin of the MacIver Campbells* — 71
- *The Origin of the Macintyres of Glennoe* — 72

Everyone Has Their Place   74
Kinship: Biological and Contractual   74
Roles and Professions   77
Land-Holding   78
Primary Sources   80
   Fosterage Contract of Tormod MacLeòid   80
   Martin Martin, A Description of the Western Isles   81
   Bonds between MacRaes and Campbells   83
   Edmund Burt, Letters from the North   84
   Rev. John Macpherson, Critical Dissertations   84
   Rev. Donald MacQueen, "A Dissertation…"   86
   Rev. John Buchanan, Travels in the Western Hebrides   87
   Anne Grant, Essays on the Superstitions and Letters   88

The Bare Necessities   92
Living in a Material World   92
Primary Sources   95
   Finlay the Red-haired Bard, "My Favorite Big-House"   95
   George Buchanan, The History of Scotland   98
   Unnamed MacLeod, "Lament for Iain mac GilleChaluim"   99
   Anonymous, A Collection of Highland Rites and Customs   100
   Martin Martin, A Description of the Western Isles   101
   Edmund Burt, Letters from the North   103
   Alasdair mac Mhaighstir Alasdair, "The Proud Plaid"   104
   Rev. John Buchanan, Travels in the Western Hebrides   107
   Sarah Murray, A Companion and Useful Guide   110
   Alexander Carmichael, "Grazing and Agrestic Customs"   111
   Mary MacKellar, "The Sheiling"   114
   Anonymous, "The Dornoch Firth"   116

From Birth to Death — 119
Rituals and Meaning — 119
- Birth — 120
- Baptism — 121
- Marriage — 121
- Death — 123

Primary Sources — 123
- Anonymous, *A Collection of Highland Rites and Customs* — 123
- Martin Martin, *A Description of the Western Isles* — 124
- Rev. John Buchanan, *Travels in the Western Hebrides* — 125
- Sir Aeneas Mackintosh, "Notes Descriptive and Historical" — 126
- John Ramsay, *Scotsmen in the Eighteenth Century* — 128
- Anne Grant, *Letters* — 131
- William Stewart, *The Popular Superstitions* — 132
- David Stewart, *Sketches of the Highlanders of Scotland* — 134
- Lilias Campbell, *Records of Argyll* — 135
- Dugald MacDougall, *Records of Argyll* — 136
- William MacKenzie, *Book of Arran* — 137

Writing A Research Paper — 139
Understanding Thesis Statements — 139
- Good and Poor Examples of Thesis Statements — 139
- Are These Thesis Statements? Why or Why Not? — 140
- Thesis Statement Checklist — 140

Research Process and Outline — 140

Bibliography — 143

About the Author — 148

Introduction

This volume provides an introductory guide to understanding the everyday life of the people who lived in the Scottish Highlands during the "Age of Clans," that is, from the twelfth to the late eighteenth century.

There are many ways in which people become interested in the history and traditions of the Scottish Highlands. Some people are acutely aware of their heritage, as their own forebears have kept the memory of it alive. Others may find out that they have Scottish Highland ancestry through family trees or DNA tests. Still others – with or without Scottish ancestors – may become interested in Highland history and culture through music, dance, romance novels, or Hollywood films. All of these are valid gateways into what often becomes a long and exciting journey into one of the most colorful and celebrated native cultures of Europe.

Most standard accounts of the Highlands, however, treat the culture and traditions of the region superficially and are biased by the anglocentric attitudes of those who came to dominate the region. It is a truism that "history is written by the winners," and the voices of the Gaelic-speaking people of the Scottish Highlands are seldom taken seriously by writers purporting to provide an account of the culture, history, and identity of the region. Even near the end of the twentieth century, the accomplished scholar John Lorne Campbell, who spent his life recording and publishing Gaelic traditions of all kinds, remarked that Highlanders are still grossly misrepresented in historical scholarship:

> Unless a historian possesses some knowledge of the Gaelic language and its written and oral literature, and has the insights that that knowledge bestows, it is very difficult not to be borne down by the accumulating weight of official assertions and propaganda, and arrive at the mental state of accepting them without question. ... Far too long have the Scottish Gaels been treated by historians as non-persons with no legitimate point of view.[1]

It is for this reason that anyone wanting to understand Scottish Highlanders needs to make use of materials created by the people themselves, reflecting their own perspectives and experiences.

Readers motivated by an interest in genealogy will appreciate that a family tree is simply a structured list of names that cannot provide insight into the daily lives of their ancestors, their sense of identity, social structures and values, or historical viewpoints. This book is meant to help satisfy curiosity about these questions and to lead to a more accurate and nuanced understanding of Highland society by prioritizing sources made by native Gaels in their own language. Allowing Scottish Highlanders to speak for themselves helps to humanize them and opens a crucial window into their own lives.

As this book gives you the opportunity to read primary sources, it begins with a chapter about the study of history and the use of documentary evidence. No source can be entirely free of subjectivity because all information comes from someone who must have had some individual point of view. This chapter also summarizes the differences of perspective that can distort sources due to divergent cultural origins and/or social classes, and provides a brief introduction to the Gaelic literary tradition which produced so many of the primary sources that survive to tell us about the past.

There are many popular misconceptions about Scotland in general and Highland identity in particular based on modern assumptions about national unity and racial definitions of ethnicity. The use of tartan and kilts to decorate the celebration of Scottish heritage in the modern era has blurred the lines between specific ethnic identities and regional cultures and made fundamental historical distinctions virtually invisible. The second chapter offers an overview of the forces that created the divisions between Highland and Lowland regions in Scotland and presents the ways in which Scots on both sides of that border have seen and expressed their diverging identities.

Names reflect personal and group identity, so the third chapter explains common naming practices in the Scottish Highlands. Given that Gaelic was the sole language of most people in the Highlands in this era, almost everyone's name was in that language. Names, and surnames in particular, have been mangled and distorted by being translated or transliterated into English, so this chapter explains some of the most common Gaelic elements that occur in Highland personal and family names. Having introduced clan names, it also offers a number of traditional nicknames for clans and sayings about them.

Stories about the founders of lineages and the mystique of having origins "beyond the mists of time" form part of the glamour of Highland clans. The fourth chapter presents the origin legends of prominent clans and discusses how we can make best use of these stories today, in order to understand their purposes and the agendas of those who wrote and told them in the past.

One of the common misconceptions about Highland society is that clans were extended families and that surnames are reliable guides to genealogy. The fifth chapter explains how clans were organized and the many types of bonds between people in the Highlands. It also discusses how clans could dynamically change their membership to meet the needs of leaders who expanded into new areas or retreated from lost territory.

Humans can only survive if we are sustained by a minimal supply of food, clothing, and shelter. The sixth chapter outlines some of the ways in which Highlanders met their basic needs in a challenging environment that left little room for error and much room for creativity and hard work.

One of the purposes of culture is to provide structure and meaning to our lives beyond the mundane and material world. In most traditional societies, life is understood to consist of a series of distinct stages, from birth to death, with the transition to each new stage being punctuated by a rite of passage. The seventh and last chapter explores the common patterns that explain these folk rituals and presents the common elements in rites of passage in Highland society.

There is an appendix at the end of the volume to help with formulating a thesis statement and undertaking a research paper on topics related to the material in this book. Although not all readers will be using this volume as a textbook in a formal course of study, understanding how research is done is a worthwhile exercise that can be applied widely by everyone in interpreting the past, present, and future.

Every chapter contains primary sources to enable you to read what people in the past – especially Highlanders themselves – said about their own lived realities. The texts are presented in chronological order. Information about the authors – when it is known – is provided in the introduction to the first text by him or her. I have tried to use texts from the clan era itself as much as possible but have had to supplement these by drawing from nineteenth century sources when they reflect accurately on earlier periods.

Although most of these texts were written by Highlanders, others were written by outsiders whose fresh eyes encourage them to record interesting details that natives might have taken for granted. Some outsiders expressed negative opinions about the Highlands and the people there, but even Highlanders themselves could be critical of native practices when they believed them to be contrary to orthodox Christianity or what they perceived to be the standards of "modernity" as defined by the English-speaking world.

I have translated several primary sources from Gaelic into English. Many others were written in various forms of English or Lowland Scots, and I have sometimes edited or adapted the text to be accessible to modern anglophone readers. I have sometimes also emended Gaelic orthography to meet modern standards. I have noted such interventions to the texts in the citations.

I am grateful to Linda Gowans for giving me digital scans of the illustration of a thatched house from Thomas Pennant's 1790 volume as well as of a postcard of peat-cutters from the early 1900s. Thanks to Scottish Gaelic speaker and artist Críostóir Piondargás for creating the map of Scotland.

---

[1] Campbell, *Canna*, ix.

Chapter 1

Studying History, Using Sources

This chapter will enable you to answer the questions:
- What types of historical research are done by modern scholars?
- What are primary and secondary sources?
- How can we best make use of sources for historical research?
- What kinds of sources exist that tell us something about the Scottish Highlands and Highlanders and what are their tradeoffs?

What is History? What is Historical Research?

The word "history" has two common usages. First and most broadly speaking, it is refers to what has happened in the past. Second, and more specifically, it refers to the study of what happened in the past and ways of interpreting it. Like other fields of scholarship, history has developed dramatically over the last several decades and historians have many choices in how they approach the study of history, who and what they study, and what they use to do so.

The past starts in the present moment and goes back infinitely. In theory, we could study what happened yesterday or a thousand years ago, although the study of history is generally understood to be grounded in textual sources (documents made up of words), even if other kinds of information (such as archaeological artifacts) can be used to complement them. One of the main tasks of the historian is to locate, identify, contextualize, and analyze the sources of information that can be used to understand the past.

The conventional – and obsolete – understanding of history is that it is a search for "truth," as though there can only be a single account of what happened in the past. Most modern historians no longer believe in this simplistic view of a unitary meaning of the past. Instead, it is now generally held to be more credible and productive to consider the many different viewpoints from which events are experienced and perceived and the many contexts in which they happen.

Society is comprised of many different agents. The agendas of these agents might relate to their personal priorities and ambitions, or be aligned to collective interests, such as their shared religion, cultural identity, etc. In researching and writing history, we can choose from many different perspectives. Assembling a wide variety of historical sources enables us to consider the many different ways in which people and communities participated in and understood the meaning of past events.

Many people still often assume that history is primarily an enumeration of dates, battles, powerful rulers, and disasters. While these are undeniably significant factors, they are not the only ones that people experience and determine the course and fabric of their lives. Our understanding of the past – our ability to understand what happened across time, space, and social groups – and of how different people understood events has been greatly improved by widening the variety of sources that are examined and increasing the diversity of people who created those sources.

Whether an event or development seems to be "good" or "bad" depends very much on the position and perspective of the individual or community in question. We can now enjoy historical studies that look at the past through such critical lenses as social class, ecology, gender, race, and religion. This has greatly enhanced our appreciation of the complexity of the human experience and our relationship to the world and to one another.

Historians also commonly attempt to identify the factors that influenced what happened in the past, that is to say, to look for patterns that explain *causality*. It is easily understood that actions in the material world, whether they are triggered by humans or natural forces, have consequences: wars, famines, plagues, migrations, and so on. These physical phenomena produce effects on people in very direct and observable ways.

It may be less obvious that concepts, beliefs, and values can also have important and lasting consequences. Societies can undergo profound changes on a number of levels – from intellectual to material – because of being exposed to and integrating a new set of ideas and practices, causing culture to be reordered, reoriented, and reshaped. To use a biological analogy, ideas are contagious and mutate to adapt to their hosts, changing their hosts in the process. Examples of such shifts include the invention of agriculture, literacy, monotheism, and private property.

Historians are constantly questioning previous interpretations of the past, although it is not only the interpretation of trained professionals that deserve our attention. Historians also seek to understand the ways in which stories about the past are constructed to serve the social and political needs of the people who create and tell them, despite or regardless of what actually happened at the times in which those stories are set. In other words, history is a field that also scrutinizes texts that purport to explain the past. We can learn a lot about the assumptions, biases, concerns, and ambitions of the interpreters of history and the societies that produced these interpretations by carefully reading the stories that they tell.

Most of us were taught, for example, that the Romans built a glorious empire that fell to an onslaught of barbarian invaders in the fifth century AD. Very few professional historians still think that this is an accurate interpretation of events, however. This story about Rome was created by the English historian Edward Gibbon in his book *Decline and Fall of the Roman Empire*, which he published in 1776, just as colonies in North America were offering the first large-scale, sustained resistance against the rule of the British empire. Gibbon's cautionary tale reflects the anxieties of the British élite as they witnessed the expansion of, and challenges to, their own vast dominion. Modern historians refute the simplistic narrative by pointing out that Roman power shifted to the east in the fourth century and lasted for many more centuries – in fact, some argue that it never fell at all in the east and that the western regions simply experienced slow and steady transformation![1]

Words are central to the representation and interpretation of history. Words are a reflection of power, of who has the ability and authority to speak for the past and the present. Those who wield these words also have the ability to project their power and influence how people in the present and future will perceive the past.

Sources: Primary and Secondary

Primary sources are created by people who witness events or participate in them, taking such forms in the modern world as diaries, notebooks, interviews, and newspaper articles. Official documents recorded by organizations or powerful people are particularly common primary sources: laws, speeches, records of meetings, correspondence, legal contracts, and so on. Primary sources also include formal records such as land grants, financial accounts, court trials, and legal proclamations.

The Scottish Highlands can be studied and understood by using the many forms of oral tradition produced by and for the native Gaelic communities who live there: song-poems, oral history, prose narratives, genealogies, proverbs, and so on. When using primary sources such as these we must consider how they were transcribed from oral tradition to the written word, by whom, for what purpose, how the text was transmitted and by whom, how the stylistic conventions of oral genres can affect its content, and so on.

Secondary sources are texts written by scholars who have researched primary sources in order to come up with their own interpretations and analyses. Most history books and articles are considered to be secondary sources, but some are actually tertiary sources because they rely not on primary evidence but are themselves drawn from secondary sources.

There has been conflict between English-speaking peoples of England and the Scottish Lowlands, on the one hand, and Gaelic-speaking peoples of the Scottish Highlands and Ireland (who call themselves *Gàidheil* "Gaels"), on the other, for many centuries. Each of these groups has their own perspectives, but the histories of Ireland and Scotland have long been dominated by English-speaking historians using sources recorded by other English-speaking people. This has meant that the perspective of the Gaels of these lands has not been taken into account properly by mainstream histories in the past, not only because few historians have had the proper linguistic skills to access them, but also because the Gaelic record in its many forms – particularly poetry and oral narrative – has not been recognized as being as valid a source as written documents in English.

A balanced interpretation of historical events can no more afford to ignore the documents recorded by English-speaking officials than they can afford to ignore the traditions recorded from the people who experienced them and were directly affected by them. The multi-lingual evidence from Scottish history is a challenge for the historian, as Scotland has always been home to a variety of peoples and languages, including various forms of Gaelic, Brittonic, Latin, Norse, and English.

The diagrams below provide impressionistic representations of the relationships between author, audience, and the human subjects represented in the primary sources about the Scottish Highlands in this era. Social groups are represented in each diagram as a pyramid: the élite (the top section), the intermediary caste (minor gentry, landholders, clergy, intelligentsia, etc., as the middle section), and the peasantry (non-landholders on the bottom). The author(s) of the source(s) are shaded. Although these diagrams depict the relations between Gaelic Highlanders and Lowlanders, the latter category could be extended to the anglophones of England and others.

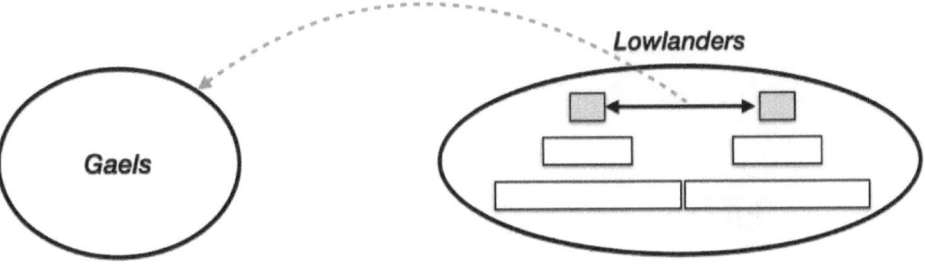

Diagram 1.1: Wholly external sources

Diagram 1.1 represents the case of sources composed by Lowland élite for other Lowland élite about Gaels, without the involvement of Gaels themselves in the creation of the texts. Even to the present day, the writing of Scottish history has been biased by entrenched and systemic stereotypes of Gaels in anglophone sources.

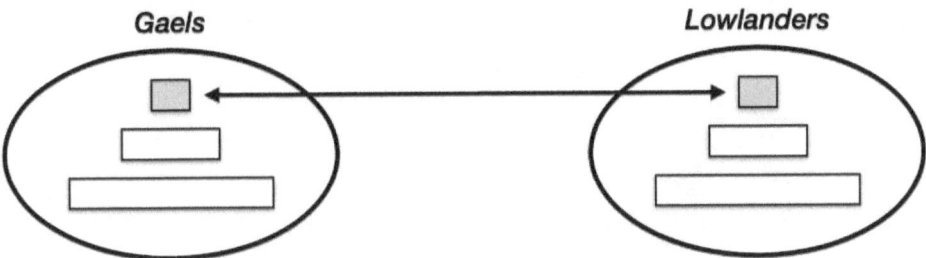

Diagram 1.2: Internal - external sources

Diagram 1.2 represents sources composed by Gaelic élite to Lowland élite, or vice-versa. Most of the Scottish élite were literate in Latin, and the Highland élite were typically literate in Latin, Gaelic, and Scots. A text that represents a dialog across communities opens the possibility of communication across cultural gaps, and hence more explicit explanation of the differences between communities. Unfortunately, however, the Lowlands tended to be strongly dominant over the Highlands, and so this power imbalance generally causes Lowland cultural and linguistic norms to be imposed on the sources. Gaelic cultural norms and perspectives can become "invisible" in such documents.

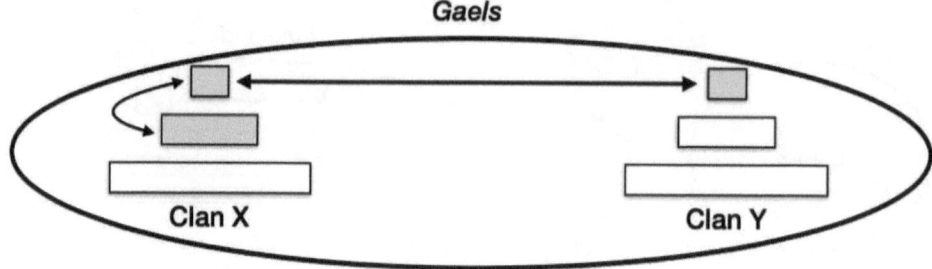

Diagram 1.3: Internal inter-élite sources

Diagram 1.3 represents sources composed by the Gaelic élite of one clan to the Gaelic élite of another kin-group, or sources composed between two members of the same clan. This kind of source is likely to tell us much more about matters internal to Gaelic society, although it may be limited to the interests of the élite and may be biased by their agendas and ambitions.

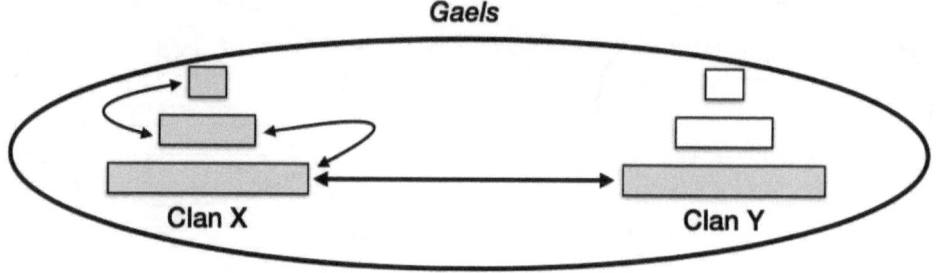

Diagram 1.4: Internal non-élite sources

Diagram 1.4 represents the kind of source we don't have in abundance until the eighteenth century or later: sources composed by non-élite Gaels representing their views, perspectives, and experiences, communicated to other Gaels of the same kin-group or another. These texts are crucial in our efforts to understand the lives – material, intellectual, emotional, and social – of Scottish Highlanders during the clan era.

Introduction to Gaelic Literary Tradition

Some of the most important primary sources in Gaelic that we have are in the form of song-poems. Before the seventeenth century, many of these are highly elaborate verses composed by highly-trained professional poets who acted like a combination of counselor, historian, and public-relations agent for clan chieftains. Until at least the seventeenth century, most chieftains with adequate wealth employed an official poet. The primary responsibilities of the trained poet were to praise the chieftain publicly, satirize his enemies, protect him from the satire of his enemies, and maintain a form of family history. The poet could also act as diplomat to the chieftain, and tutor to his children and those of related nobility.

If this poet had the full training of the poetic schools – about seven years in length – he was called a *file* (*filidh* is the plural form). This was a qualification like "Ph.D.," and the title of his position as official poet to a chieftain was *ollamh*. There were also lesser poets (*bard* singular, *baird* plural) that did not have as much formal education and did not expect as high of a salary. It was probably also the case in Scotland that only the major western clans most strongly connected with Ireland – MacDonalds, Campbells, MacLeans, and MacLeods – kept a *file*.

The high-register poetry of the *file* was a kind of public statement about his patron's right to rule, a sort of oral charter for leadership:

> a qualified poet's praise of a chieftain was a kind of certificate (poet's truth, *fír filidh*) in support of the legitimacy of the patron's right to rule. ... More practically, in the high middle ages and early modern period, if a poet became known as issuing indiscriminate praise that had no relation to the real qualities of the patron, it devalued his status, and potentially his ability to demand a high price for his endorsement of a magnate.[2]

This legitimation of the ruler was based on formal principles as well as cultural precedents understood and shared by the audience who were present at important rituals of leadership, such as inaugurations.

The high social status of the *file* made him very visible and influential in Gaelic society. The products of his work – the praise and satire of human subjects, especially his patron and his patron's family – had a strong impact on the style of Gaelic literature of all kinds. John MacInnes has argued that the clan poets produced an internally consistent literary style which reflects the heroic ethos of medieval Highland society and its struggle to survive against the opposition of the anglophone central government of the Lowlands and, later, London.

These literary conventions, which MacInnes named the "panegyric code," celebrate the hero-warrior as a social leader, locate him within his genealogical lineage and territorial rights, describe the attributes, training, and accomplishments which demonstrate his right to rule, and ascribe numerous allies and social support networks to him (including God). The elements of the panegyric code[3] are primarily used in order to praise the subject. These elements, when shown to be lacking, imply that the loss of leadership creates a breach in social conventions, which implies a potential social crisis. In reverse, these literary conventions can be used to satirize a subject.

These various aspects of the Gaelic panegyric code are used primarily to praise or satirize a human subject in eulogies, elegies, lampoons, and so on, but they also appear in other literary genres that discuss people, places, and things. As John MacInnes has argued, the influence of the clan poet and his verbal artistry has been pervasive throughout the Gaelic literary tradition, not least because of the high status and prestige of the poet and the subjects for whom he composed his work.

Figure 1.5: A nineteenth-century depiction of a chieftain's hall in earlier times

The impression that the old Gaelic poets flatter and paint false portraits of their subjects jars the expectations of many modern readers. The Gaelic panegyric code should be seen, however, as not strictly a means of describing a particular person, thing or event literally, but as a system of articulating and representing the ideals of Gaelic society. A subject is described, particularly in elegies, not just as his mundane self but as an idealized reflection of his potential according to the aspirations of Gaelic society, especially as articulated by the poets.

> In very simple terms, the (panegyric) code was designed to present the subject of the poem as being, or destined or suitable to be, the 'right ruler'; the picture given was not intended to be an actual representation, but rather the model towards which the ruler should strive. ... among the most crucial of these conventional images is that of the individual as the one who can unite and lead his people, as the protector of his people and territory.[4]

It was not natural for Gaelic poets, or probably for most poets working in an oral-dominant tradition, to discuss qualities or virtues in the abstract. Instead, qualities, virtues, and vices are usually given concrete form. While a chieftain, for example, might be praised as an effective leader using adjectives like *ceannsalach* ("authoritative, fit for rule"), it is more common, and must have been thought more convincing, to portray him at the helm of a ship with the implicit understanding that it is the ship of state that he was steering.

If we wish to gain a deep understanding of a person or event as represented in Gaelic literature, we need to take into account the ways in which the language, style, and rhetoric of the literary tradition has influenced what the poet says and how he or she says it. Determining the message a poet has encoded in a piece of poetry requires understanding how literary devices are used, why one device is used rather than another, how the poet draws upon symbols, phrases, characters, plots, and motifs familiar from other texts, and what the poet leaves unstated despite it being prescribed by convention. This requires being familiar with the wider corpus of Gaelic literature.

> There is an important social and political message, then, embedded in the poetry. Essential to the modern reader is the need to keep sight of the fact that this message is conveyed in codified diction, so that interpreting quite literally a poet's words can lead to serious error. The listing of allies so common in vernacular verse is one typical example: what we have here is rather the listing of potential allies, because this is a mere propaganda device. And so, while factual historical information can be found in Gaelic poetry, the reader must interpret the code before attempting to establish what constitutes a clean statement of fact. It should further be borne in mind that not infrequently poetic discourse is affected by metrical requirements.[5]

Gaelic poets generally represent themselves as truth-tellers and their verbal artistry as a direct and straightforward expression of personal experience and/or that of their communities. The reality is more complicated. The community looked to the poet as someone who was articulate and would take a stand on important issues. We can often see the poet acting like a lawyer or minister advocating a particular cause or speaking on behalf of a particular person or group. We also see him or her trying to make sense of complex issues on behalf of the community, or rallying the community in the face of future challenges.

Although the lower echelons of Gaelic society were not taught to read or write until the eighteenth century or later, the higher ranks – the *filidh* and the clergy – wrote down at least some of their literary output by the seventh century, even if most of it was never recorded. Poems in praise of patrons were those most likely to be written down, as they were had a clear social function and financial reward. Poetry composed by the lower ranks of society circulated in oral tradition until it was transcribed by literate men, mostly church ministers.

It is to be expected that items survive in oral transmission if they continue to have purpose and value to the community. In the course of oral transmission, however, the poet's words might be further elaborated, new words inserted, or original words removed, in order to reflect ongoing interpretations of the past, present, and future. Even the community in which it has been preserved may have forgotten, misconstrued, or reinvented the *seanchas* (lore and stories) associated with the text.

We must be cautious about assuming that song-poems and prose narratives about events were composed at the same time they describe by eye-witnesses; it is certainly possible for texts to be composed long afterward, with the events and people portrayed taking on added significance in retrospect.

On top of the historical information it contains, the verbal artistry of Scottish Highlanders is worthy of our attention because it was considered the most important form of cultural expression that they produced, the very culmination of their powers of creativity. The professional poet was held in the highest esteem – just below that of the clan leaders that he served – and even accomplished village poets were treated with the greatest regard and esteem. While some cultures focused their efforts on producing splendor in architecture, portraiture, sculpture, and so on, literature is the most important and revered form of expression in the Gaelic world, and anyone wanting to understand the lives and worldview of their Highland ancestors cannot afford to neglect it.

Gaelic oral tradition – of all genres, but particularly song-poetry – was constantly present in the life of Scottish Highlanders, like being permanently tuned into a radio station that pervaded their thoughts about their sense of history, identity, and virtue. Almost every task of their day was accompanied by songs that connected them to the people and events of their past and kept anchored them to their own culture, regardless of where they lived, including as immigrants in distant lands.

Reading Sources Critically

If you wish to study primary sources to interpret what they might reveal about the past, it is crucial that you ask the appropriate questions and apply the relevant methods. Even if you cannot answer all of the questions below definitively, keeping them in mind will help you to maintain a skeptical approach to primary sources and encourage you to ask questions that force you to "read between the lines."[6]

Authorship and Origin

- Who is the author? What is his/her ethnic identity, gender, social class, profession, political allegiance, religious denomination, etc?
- How might the author's identity influence the text?
- When and where was this text created?
- Did somebody other than the author of the text transcribe or edit it? How might the line of transmission of the text have altered its content?

Subjects, Content and Context

- Who and what is this text about?
- Who and what are the people, places, and events named in this text? Why are they named? What is their significance?
- How does the text reflect (or contradict) historical circumstances known from other sources?

Genre

- In what literary or historical tradition was this text composed?
- How has the genre of the text affected the rhetoric and style?
- If this is a song-poem, is it based on a previous song-poem whose meaning adds to this one by implied allusion?

Agenda and Argument

- What is the agenda of the author/document? Summarize it briefly.

- How does the text rationalize the agenda? In other words, by what logic does it justify its agenda?
- Who is the intended audience of the text? How might this influence its rhetorical strategy?

Interpretations

- How might this text support or contradict one of the arguments found in a secondary source?
- What kinds of information does this text reveal that it does not seemed concerned with revealing? In other words, what does it tell us without knowing it's telling us?
- If this text is a literary text, can it be read as an allegory or parable making a veiled comment about contemporary people and events?
- If this text purports to be an historical document (describing the past), has its representation of and commentary about things in the more distant past been influenced by contemporary (more recent) people and events?

Inter-relations Between Primary Sources

- Is the text making allusion to other texts ("inter-textuality")? How might other related texts shed light on this one by comparison and contrast?
- What patterns or ideas are repeated throughout the sources?
- What major differences appear between them?
- What do the differences between sources relate to? Do they reflect different social groups, personal/familial ambitions, political allegiances, religious doctrines, or other factors?

---

[1] Pilkington, "Five myths about the decline and fall of Rome."

[2] Simms, *Medieval Gaelic sources*, 68-9.

[3] Organized hierarchically in Newton, *Warriors of the Word*, 116-18.

[4] Coira, *By Poetic Authority*, 27.

[5] Ibid, xi-xii.

[6] Much of this list has been adapted from https://courses.bowdoin.edu/writing-guides/

Chapter Two

Divide and Conquer
Highland-Lowland Distinctions

This chapter will enable you to answer the questions:
- When and how did the Highland clan system evolve?
- How and why did the division between Highlands and Lowlands emerge? What did it signify?
- How did Highlanders and Lowlanders think about their identities?

Feudal Scotland

The "Highland clan system," if we can use the term loosely, emerged as Gaelic kindreds and communities of the Scottish mainland responded to the introduction of Anglo-Norman practices of government and socio-economic structures in the twelfth century. This had wide-ranging impacts throughout Scotland and eventually resulted in a geographical and ethnic division between Highlands and Lowlands. A short historical summary is necessary to explain how these developments led to an ethnic division along geographical boundaries, so that Highlands and Lowlands came to reflect a fundamental fault-line in Scotland.

At the time of the Norman invasion in England (1066), the Gaelic language and culture was at its high-water mark across the mainland of Scotland: Gaelic was the language of the courts of the king and most of the native aristocrats; it was used by the church clergy and learned people; it was the common tongue of communities in the south of Scotland, even south of the river Tweed (as place names demonstrate).[1] Scottish identity and culture was understood to be built on a Gaelic foundation, even if other ethnic enclaves – Brittonic peoples, Anglo-Saxons, Norse – were also incorporated as subjects of the king.

One of the most momentous changes in Scotland's history was the marriage of King Malcolm III to the Anglo-Saxon princess Margaret in 1070. The new queen strongly preferred her own culture and social norms and took action to privilege them in Scotland. Their youngest son, David, was raised as a hostage in the French-speaking court of Henry I of

England, the son of William the Conqueror, and was said to have been a paragon of Norman knighthood. David ruled as "the prince of the Cumbrian region" (made up of Strathclyde, Tweeddale and Teviotdale) during the reign of his older brother Alexander I. He brought new forms of secular and religious government into that area and relied heavily upon them after ascending to the Scottish throne in 1124.[2]

David imposed a broad range of political, economic and religious changes on Scotland that gets bundled up in the term "feudalism." Previous generations of historians tended to present feudalism as though it was a uniform set of cultural, economic, and political policies. In fact, a feudal facade often obscured a diverse set of social structures and practices. This was true for Scotland as well, as native customs could be expressed in terms of "feudal" concepts.[3] The principles and practices associated with feudal society, as defined by the Anglo-Normans, can be generalized as follows:

- The king is the absolute owner of all land and directly appoints the holders of all offices.
- The commendation ceremony: the king accepts a vassal with an act of homage and oath of fealty, giving absolute loyalty and submission to his superiority.
- The king grants land charters to vassals.
- Vassals must provide military services to the king.
- Lords (under the king) are invested with estates and power over an unfree population on those estates.
- Primogeniture: the first-born male heir inherits office, there is no subdivision of property to other sons.
- Military strongholds are ruled by knights to enforce the king's rule.
- The king grants economic privileges and duties to boroughs (called "burghs" in Scotland) to create an economic infrastructure controlled by the king which produces income for him.

Under this feudal arrangement, although the king was the absolute overlord of all his people, his rule still required careful diplomacy with lower tiers of society in order for maintain effective rule.

Rather than being entirely new developments, the Anglo-Norman settlement intensified trends already underway in Scotland: there was already an English-speaking population in the south-east; permanent urban settlements trading with international partners were already in place and gaining economic importance; church institutions were in the process of being reformed by mainstream continental religious orders; and the

Scottish Crown had long been trying to consolidate its power and downgrade regional leaders and national rivals.[4]

This era is complicated to understand because of the influx into Scotland of new people and concepts about society and politics, and the shifting balance of power and culture in various regions at different times: incomers used feudal structures to their own advantage in some circumstances, or assimilated into Gaelic structures in others; native Scots sought to benefit by adapting feudal structures in some circumstances, resisted the foreign influx in others, or aided the king to put down "rebellions" against these changes, seeking to enrich themselves in the process. This warns us against seeing political events and processes in purely ethnic terms.

Regardless, we should not underestimate the effects (especially on language and culture) of elevating the prestige of French culture and English-speakers in Scotland at the expense of Gaelic.

> The influence of David's 'French' subjects in defining the shape and future of aristocratic life in late medieval Scotland may have been far greater than their absolute numbers might suggest. Most significantly, of course, the Scottish royal house had itself became a centre of Frankish culture, language and attitudes, an adopted position reinforced by the marriage policies of the dynasty for the remainder of the twelfth century and international developments in the cult of kingship. ... political, social and cultural domination could be achieved by means other than outright military conquest.[5]

Once the feudal structures and mechanisms were in place, regardless of the ethnicity of those responsible for implementing or accepting them, they could be used to leverage the power of the king and to cause cultural, linguistic, and ethnic allegiances to trickle down to all of his subjects.

The use of such political mechanisms to hold and exercise power gave the royal dynasty greater reach and power in extending their authority over the realm, ousting rivals and consolidating their hold on power. This coincided with the narrowing down of the members of the royal family in Scotland and elsewhere in Britain.

A *burgh* was a legal entity recognized by the king which privileged a community of burgesses with the right to trade and gave them exemption from toll charges throughout the kingdom. About fifteen burghs were founded during David's reign (1124–1153), largely populated by Flemish immigrants. King William the Lion (reign 1165–1214) later granted the first burghal charters.

Most Scottish burghs were in the south and east, where they had access to natural resources and sea routes that enabled them to trade with the continent of Europe. By the mid-fourteenth century, burgesses had a place in the Scottish Parliament alongside churchmen and the nobility, making them one of the "three estates."[6] The economic and political importance of burghs gave them a greater prestige than Gaelic-speaking rural villages. Besides coming to sell raw materials and buy finished products, Gaelic speakers came to the burghs for employment, not least because the high mortality rate in towns from disease, fires, and warfare created demand to replace the lost population with immigrants.[7]

A language then called "Inglis" by its speakers (but later called "Scots") emerged from the mixture of languages of earlier Anglo-Saxon settlements, the Flemish mercantile class, Anglo-Norman élite, and Northern English subjects who were brought in during the feudal reform. The use of Inglis for commerce and administration in the burghs enabled its spread through Lowland Scotland at the expense of Gaelic.

Highlands and Lowlands

It was much easier for King David I, and his successors after him, to impose feudalism in the Lowlands and consolidate power there than doing so in the Highlands. For one, Scotland was not an entirely unified, centralized kingdom, and leaders in areas such as Galloway, Ross, and the Western and Northern Isles fought against the encroachments of the Scottish Crown and for their own sovereignty. Second, the Highlands were not as a whole suitable for high-yield agriculture in the same way as the Lowlands, so it was not feasible to plant burghs that could be filled with colonists loyal to the king. Not only were foreigners unfamiliar with the landscape but the movement of goods and armies was difficult and required intimate knowledge of the rough terrain. Along the western seaboard and in the Western Isles, travel was almost exclusively restricted to boats using lochs and sea-ways. It was difficult for the eastern, landlocked Anglo-Normans to compete with people who had developed marine technologies suited to the watery environment.

Nonetheless, the Anglo-Norman power of feudalism was expanding from the Lowlands and straining to extend itself throughout Scotland on behalf of the dynasty descended from Malcolm Canmore. The social, economic, and political implications meant that the Gaels of the

Highlands and Western Isles had to adapt to changing circumstances and defend themselves against the agents of the Crown by creating their own version of feudalism. Although there were continuities in Gaelic society that went back to the Iron Age, the "clan system" should not be seen as an ancient order predating feudalism but a response to it, as the leaders in the Highlands found ways to adapt innovations to enhance their own power and social stability.

Although feudal innovations had the effect of assimilating native Gaels into an Inglis society in the Lowlands, Anglo-Normans quickly learned Gaelic, and assimilated to Gaelic norms, in areas where the culture remained strong, particularly the Highlands. Many large clans, such as the Chisholms, the Frasers, the Grants, the Menzies, and the Stewarts, were founded by Anglo-Norman settlers who married into Gaelic communities and had to accommodate the local culture to be accepted by their dependents.

Similarly, the Norse settled in the Western Isles and the Isle of Man, and along the western seaboard of the Highlands, became Gaelicized and integrated into Gaelic society during the first few centuries of the feudal era. The imperative to become fully Gaelicized was so strong that nearly all clans altered their family trees to claim descent from Gaelic founders, even when clan names are transparently Norse, as is demonstrated by such surnames as *MacAsgaill* ("MacAskill," "MacCaskill," etc.), *MacIomhair* ("MacIver"), and *MacThorcaill* ("MacCorkill," "MacCorkle," etc.).

This attests to the resilience and self-confidence of Gaelic culture, encompassing both Ireland and much of mainland Scotland at the time: "these shifts must have been deliberate, with Gaelic identity being consciously promoted and Scandinavian connections consciously discarded and disregarded."[8] The only exception to this was the MacLeods (*Clann 'ic Leòid*), whose poets continued to proclaim descent from a Norse founder despite these social pressures.

Although there were battles, invasions, and population displacements with significant consequences, change throughout Scotland would likely have seemed gradual to many of those alive at the time. The consequences, however, were such that Lowland Scotland was being assimilated into anglophone culture and becoming estranged from its Gaelic origins. By the late fourteenth century, Scotland became polarized into two cultural and geographical zones — Highland and Lowland — whose inhabitants viewed each other with suspicion if not hostility.

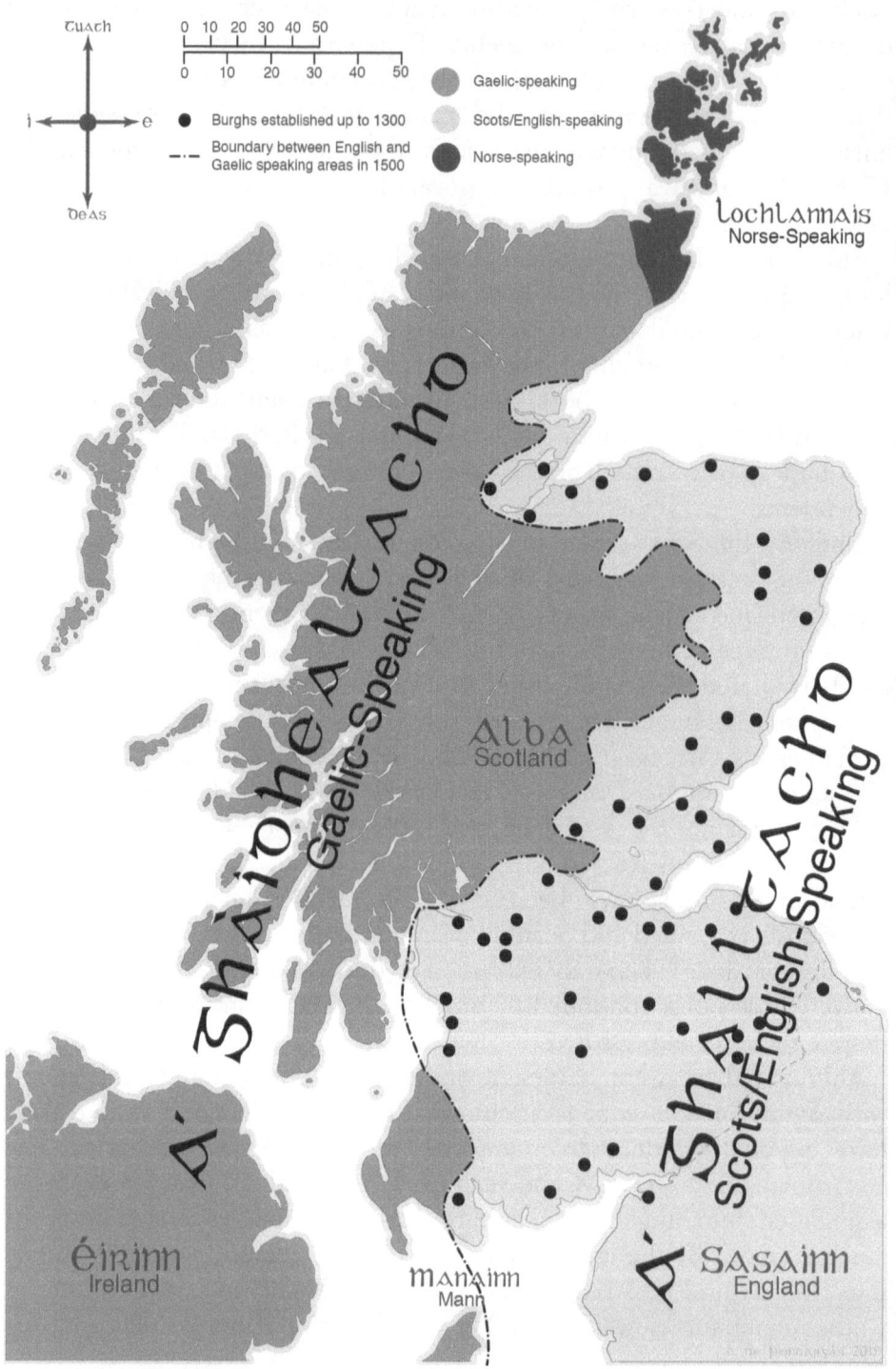

Identity and Ethnicity

The term "ethnicity" refers to the identity of social groups and communities, perceptions of being united as a group and different from others. Race and biology have become the dominant ways in which people in the modern world think about identity, but people in the past have understood similarities and differences to be based on a range of other factors. Communities throughout history have forged a common, unifying identity based on shared cultural practices and beliefs – such as language, religion, myths, and rituals – as well as geography. We could say, then, that ethnicity is created by communities from how and where they live. Identity is not static but dynamic, always in flux and responding to contemporary needs and circumstances.

Identity is contrastive by nature: defining who we are is only possible by differentiating ourselves from those who we are not. One productive way of thinking about group identity is by visualizing expanding and inclusive rings of communities, from small, intimate groups (such as family or neighborhood) to larger, more abstract ones (such as state or nation). The level of identity that is relevant to us may depend on context as much as any real characteristics. An American from California traveling abroad in Italy, for example, may bond easily with someone they encounter from Louisiana due to their common ethnicity as Americans, yet that Californian may feel greater affinity with someone from the same state if they were to visit New Orleans on another occasion.

Ethnicity is closely related to culture in that cultural practices, beliefs, and values are often why groups see themselves as being distinctive. Ethnicity does not necessarily have to rely upon massive differences in culture, however, because ethnicity is about perception and a collective consensus of ideas about identity. What may seem to be insignificant to an outsider may be the cause of heated division between groups.

Historians and archeologists warn us time and again not to confuse biological descent with ethnicity. The historical summary above has already indicated how people from varying origins can assimilate and be absorbed into differing ethnic communities: Norse and Anglo-Norman settlers became Gaelicized in the west and the Gaels of the Lowlands were absorbed into Inglis-speaking burghs. Even smaller kin-groups often fabricated parts of their genealogies to graft themselves inside of the family structures of clans to whom they gave their allegiance.[9]

Somewhat ironically, DNA evidence is actually providing further evidence that genes and identity are entirely different matters. A recent archaeological study investigating artifacts and DNA from a port city on the Mediterranean coast of Israel, a strong hold of the Philistines, offers just one example of this. The Philistines were bitter enemies of the Israelites whose exact origin has long been debated. In the Hebrew Bible, they were said to descend from Caluhim of Egypt. The research of modern archaeology instead indicates that there was a short burst of migration from the northern coast of the European mediterranean between Greece and Spain in about the twelfth century BCE. Within a few generations, the Philistines had become so thoroughly intermingled with the local population that their genetic distinctions were barely detectable. They seem to have erased their history as migrants from Europe, instead preferring to depict themselves as settlers from Egypt.

> The findings are a good reminder, Feldman says, that a person's culture or ethnicity is not the same as their DNA. "In this situation, you have foreign people coming in with a slightly different genetic makeup, and their influence, genetically, is very short. It doesn't leave a long-lasting impact, but culturally they made an impact that lasted for many years."[10]

Many other such research projects are yielding similar results.

It's also important to recognize that identities are not exclusive at the personal level. Throughout history, human beings have had multiple ethnic identities; the one that is most relevant may depend on the community in which they are living or operating. For example, Scottish king Robert Bruce had a father who belonged to the Anglo-Norman élite of Scotland but a mother who was rooted in the local Gaelic community of Carrick. Bruce leveraged both of these ethnic identities at various times in his career, depending on where he was and what he was doing.

It is more productive to think of ethnicity as something that is defined by and belongs to communities. Individual humans can identify with multiple ethnic groups and have differing roles in each of those in which they participate. These multiple identities, the degree to which people identify with them, and the meaning of them can shift dramatically throughout a person's lifetime.

Language is also key to understanding the ethnic divisions between Highlands and Lowlands. Language is the medium through which many aspects of culture and identity are communicated and a great deal of culture is encoded in language itself. It is not surprising, then, that language is a symbolic marker of ethnic identity that often corresponds directly to the name that a people use to identify themselves as an ethnic group.

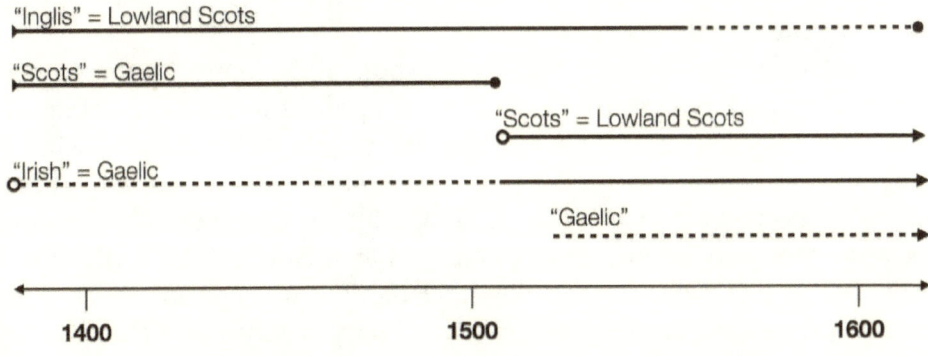

Diagram 2.2: Names used over time for the languages of Scotland

The term "Scot" originally referred to Gaelic speakers, whether living in Scotland or Ireland, and their language. The form of English spoken in the Lowlands was originally referred to as "Inglis" by speakers of that language, and this name continued to be used into the seventeenth century.

Shifts in identity caused new terms to appear and old terms to be reassigned new meanings in the language of the Lowlands. As the Gaelic-speaking Scots were closely associated with the Irish, on account of the language they spoke as well as their culture and legendary origins, Lowland anglophones began to apply the term "Irish" (especially in the form "Erse") to them in the 1380s. Although "Scotice" was used for Gaelic as late as 1505, Gaelic was generally referred to as "Irish" thereafter. From the 1520s on, Lowland writers also made occasional use of terms derived from Gaelic's name for itself. The first known use of the term "Scot" to refer to the Germanic language of the Lowlands appeared in 1494 and became the dominant term in the sixteenth century.

The native Gaels of Scotland and Ireland refer to themselves as *Gàidheil* (plural, *Gàidheal* singular). They came to call the foreigners who were settled among them – whether Norse settlers or Anglo-Norman colonists – as *Goill* (plural, *Gall* singular). By the opening of the feudal era, Gaelic literature and communal experience framed a bitter, binary opposition between *Gàidheil* and *Goill*, originally based on conflict with the Norse but later extended to Lowlanders.

The communities where Gaels live or have lived historically as a whole is referred to in Gaelic as *Gàidhealtachd* (or *a' Ghàidhealtachd* with the definite article). This corresponds approximately to the Highlands of the mainland

and the Western Isles, although there are parts of the geographical Lowlands in areas such as Stirlingshire that were Gaelic-speaking into the twentieth century. Gaels refer to the communities where Lowland anglophones live or have lived historically as a whole as *Galltachd* (or *a' Ghalltachd* with the definite article).

Within a few centuries of the colonization of Scotland by the feudal order, the boundary between Gaels and anglophones in Scotland stabilized and hardened, corresponding closely to the Highland-Lowland geographical divide. We need to recognize, on the one hand, that these were very distinct communities with different languages, cultural practices, social norms, and historical perspectives that usually treated each other with distrust if not disdain. On the other hand, it was not uncommon for some individuals (especially noblemen) to have a sense of belonging to both communities and for powerful families and dynasties to straddle both sides of the divide.

It must also be emphasized that while we use the two terms "Highlander" and "Gael" in English, both of these meanings are implied by the single word *Gàidheal* in Gaelic itself. Throughout the Middle Ages and up to the later nineteenth century, it could generally be assumed that someone living in the Highlands (a Highlander) was also a member of the ethnic Gaelic community (a Gael) whose native tongue was the Gaelic language. The people of the Highlands only started to lose their language and culture, and to be assimilated into the anglophone world, on a large scale in the later nineteenth century due to the hostile policies of the central government: the use of the educational system to destroy the Gaelic language and replace it with English, the economic dependency of the Highlands on immigration and seasonal migration for employment, and the stigmatization of all things Gaelic.[11]

Primary Sources

Unknown, *Lebor Bretnach* "The Book of Britain"

Medieval European scholars felt compelled to provide an account of the origin and lineage of ethnic groups, often grafting ancestral figures onto stories from the Bible as well as Greek and Roman sources. In about the year 829 a Welsh cleric wrote the Latin volume *Historia Brittonum* ("The History of the Britons") to provide an account of the early history and peoples of Britain. As one of the only such texts available, it was highly influential.

Some of the characters and plot lines relating to the history of the Gaels given in *Historia Brittonum* were apparently borrowed from Gaelic scholars who were already working on their own origin myth. In the eleventh century a version of *Historia Brittonum* was translated into Gaelic and given further elaborations, resulting in a text called *Lebor Bretnach* ("The British Book"). Recent scholarship has suggested that this work was carried out by scholars in Scotland, probably in St Andrews or Abernethy.[12]

The following excerpt of the tale of the origins of the Gaels remained well known into the modern period and allusions to it abound in Gaelic literature into the twentieth century. The passages given here summarize the arrival of the Gaels in Ireland and then, following the conquest of Pictish territory by the Gaelic kingdom of Dál Riata, in Scotland. We need to treat this story more as mythic narrative than an accurate portrayal of actual historical events.

§ 14. Of the History of the Gaels. Gaelic scholars give the following account of the history of their leaders in ancient times. There was a certain (Scythian) nobleman who had been banished out of the kingdom of Scythia who was in exile in Egypt. After the children of Israel passed through the Red Sea and (the Pharaoh) Forann was drowned along with his army, the Egyptians who survived banished this nobleman, because he was the son-in-law of Forann who had drowned. The Scythian and his children went into Africa, to the altars of the Philistines, to the wells of Salmara, between Rusicade (Skikda) and the Azariea Mountains, across the River Malvam, through the Mediterranean to the pillars of Hercules, beyond the Tyrrhenian Sea to Spain. They were thereafter called "the sons of Míl."

Then, a thousand and two years after Forann was drowned in the Red Sea, the sons of Míl came to Ireland in thirty boats, with thirty couples in each boat. The king, Donn, was drowned at (a place now called) "the House of Donn."

Until that time Ireland was ruled by three goddesses named Fódla, Banba, and Éire. The sons of Míl conquered them in three battles and afterwards took the kingdom. The two sons of Míl started arguing fiercely between themselves about the kingdom until their judge Amergin of the white knee, also the son of Míl, settled the dispute. He was also their poet. This is how he made peace: Ireland was divided into two halves; Éber took the south and Éremon took the north. Their descendants still live in this island.

§15. The Britons took possession of this island (Britain) in the third age of the world. The Gaels took possession of Ireland in the fourth age of the world. In this same era the Picts took the north of Britain. The people of Dál Riata came in the sixth age and took possession of Pictish territory and at that same time the Saxons conquered a portion of the territory of the Britons.[13]

Unknown, *Chronicles of the Scottish People*

The following excerpt is from an account of Scottish history written by the late fourteenth-century historian John of Fordun (near modern-day Aberdeen). This text was long assumed to have been written by him but scholars now believe that he was quoting an even earlier source. This text is, then, an early suggestion of geographical and ethnic divisions within Scotland but one based more on stereotypes than on social realities.

The character of the Scots however varies with the differences in language, for two languages are spoken amongst them, the Scottish (Gaelic) and the Teutonic (English). The people who speak the Teutonic language occupy the coastal and lowland regions, while the people who speak the Scottish language inhabit the mountains and outlying islands. The coastal people are docile and civilized, trustworthy, long-suffering, and courteous, decent in their dress, polite, and peaceable, devout in their worship, but always ready to resist injuries threatened by their enemies.

The island and mountain people, however, are fierce and untamable, uncouth and unpleasant, much given to theft, fond of doing nothing, but their minds are quick to learn, and cunning. They are strikingly handsome in appearance, but their clothing is unsightly. They are always hostile and savage not only towards the English people and language but also towards their fellow Scots because of the difference in language. They are, however, faithful and obedient to the king and kingdom, and easily made to submit to law, if rule is exerted over them.[14]

The Declaration of Arbroath

The document that has come to be known as "The Declaration of Arbroath" in the last few generations was a letter written in Latin to the Pope in 1320 asserting Scotland's independence from England. What is often overlooked about the text is that the distinctiveness of Scotland's identity is underlined by recounting the Gaelic origin legend, which forms the beginning of the document. It corresponds very closely to the story from the *Lebor Bretnach* given previously above.

> Most Holy Father, we know and from the chronicles and books of the ancients we find that among other famous nations our own, the Scots, has been graced with widespread renown. It (our nation) journeyed from Greater Scythia by way of the Tyrrhenian Sea and the Pillars of Hercules, and dwelt for a long course of time in Spain among the most savage peoples, but nowhere could it be subdued by any people, however barbarous.
>
> Thence it came, twelve hundred years after the people of Israel crossed the Red Sea, to its home in the west where it still lives today. The Britons it first drove out, the Picts it utterly destroyed, and, even though very often assailed by the Norwegians, the Danes and the English, it took possession of that home with many victories and untold efforts; and, as the histories of old time bear witness, they have held it free of all servitude ever since. In their kingdom there have reigned one hundred and thirteen kings of their own royal stock, the line unbroken by a single foreigner.[15]

John Mair, *The History of Greater Britain*

The historian and philosopher John Mair (1467–1550) published *Historia Majoris Britanniae* ("The History of Greater Britain") in 1521. In this extract (translated from Latin into English), he follows the rhetoric of John of Fordun by drawing a sharp distinction between the people of the Highlands and those of the Lowlands. It is significant, however, that Mair further divides the Highlanders into those who are materially productive and obedient to royal authority, and others who are dedicated to hunting, indolence, and "evil" ways of life. Mair also notes how widely Gaelic was spoken, saying that it had been the majority language of Scotland not long before (even if referring to Scottish Gaelic as "Irish").

> Further, just as among the Scots we find two distinct tongues, so we likewise find two different ways of life and conduct. For some are born in the forests and mountains of the north, and these we call men of the Highland, but the others men of the Lowland. By foreigners the former are called Wild Scots, the latter house-holding Scots. The Irish tongue is in use among the former, the English tongue among the latter. One-half of Scotland speaks Irish, and all these as well as the Islanders we reckon

to belong to the Wild Scots. In dress, in the manner of their outward life, and in good morals, for example, these come behind the house-holding Scots – yet they are not less, but rather much more, prompt to fight; and this both because, born as they are in the mountains, and dwellers in forests, their very nature is more combative ...

One part of the Wild Scots have a wealth of cattle, sheep, and horses, and these, with a thought for the possible loss of their possessions, yield more willing obedience to the courts of law and the king. The other part of these people delight in the chase and a life of indolence; and their chiefs eagerly follow bad men if only they may not have the need to labour; taking no pains to earn their own livelihood, they live upon others, and follow their own worthless and savage chief in all evil courses sooner than they will pursue an honest industry. They are full of mutual dissensions, and war rather than peace is their natural condition ...

Our house-holding Scots, or quiet and civil-living people – that is, all who lead a decent and reasonable life – these men hate, on account of their differing speech, as much as they do the English ...

At the present day almost the half of Scotland speaks the Irish tongue, and not so long ago it was spoken by the majority of us ...[16]

George Buchanan, *The History of Scotland*

George Buchanan (1506-82) was a Scottish scholar and historian who was trained in Paris, where he was influenced by the emerging movements of Humanism and the Reformation. Although a native Gaelic speaker from Killearn in Stirlingshire, his adherence to Latin learning gave him a negative attitude about vernacular languages such as Gaelic. He published *Rerum Scoticarum Historia* ("The History of Scotland") in 1582, shortly before he died. In the first portion of this extract (translated from Latin to English), he remarks on the polarization between *Gàidheal* and *Gall*, and the role of language in symbolizing this conflict.

A great part of this country (Galloway) still uses its ancient language. These three nations (Wales, Cornwall, Scotland), which posses, the whole coast of Britain that looks toward Ireland, preserve the indelible marks of Gallic speech and affinity. But it is worthy of particular notice, that the ancient Scots divided all the nations who inhabited Britain, into two classes, the one they called *Gàidheal*, the other *Gall*.

But our dispute is not concerning the purity and elegance of the Latin language, for, which regard to this, it is of little consequence how the British formerly pronounced their letters; the question is, how did the Latin enunciate British, not how did the British enunciate Latin sounds? As for myself, I would rather choose to remain ignorant of the barbarous dialect of the ancient Britons, than unlearn that knowledge of the Latin tongue which I acquired, when a boy, with such great labour.

I can perceive, without regret, the gradual extinction of the ancient Scottish language, and cheerfully allow its harsh sounds to die away, and give place to the softer and more harmonious tones of the Latin. For if, in this transmigration into another language, it is necessary that we yield up one thing or other, let us pass from rusticity and barbarism, to culture and civilisation, and let our choice and judgement, repair the infelicity of our birth. Or, if our labour and industry can avail in such a case, let us exert them in polishing the Greek and Latin languages, which the greater part of the world has publicly received, and in wiping away whatever stain of barbaric speech may still adhere to them.[17]

Thomas Morer, *A Short Account of Scotland*

Thomas Morer was an Englishman who served as chaplain to a Scottish regiment. He wrote a short account of Scotland in 1689 for an English audience. This excerpt highlights the ethnic divide between Lowlands and Highlands in Scotland, as well as the disdainful opinions that anglophones held about Gaels.

Scotland is distinguished into High-lands and Low-lands. …

… too many not only retain the Irish language, but the Irish religion; and not a few profess no religion at all, but are next door to barbarity and heathenism. …

Once or twice a year, great numbers of 'em get together and made a descent into the Low-lands, where they plunder the inhabitants, and so return back and disperse themselves. And this they are apt to do in the profoundest peace, it being not only natural to 'em to delight in rapine, but they do it on a kind of principle, and in conformity to the prejudice that they continually have to the Low-landers, whom they generally take for so many enemies.[18]

William Buchanan, *The Family of Buchanan*

William Buchanan of Auchmar († 1747) wrote this account of his family's origins no later than 1723. His reference to the "Milesian" descent of families is a reference to the legendary founder of the Gaels, Mîl (also called "Maoileas"), in the traditional origin legend. He also mentions Gathelus, after whom the Gaelic language was named in these tales. His account demonstrates that even families along the southern boundary of the Highlands affirmed the traditional rooting of their clans according to established Gaelic tradition, preserving a conceptual unity between the ancient families of Scotland and Ireland.

> These Ó Cathains, with some others of the most ancient and reputed Irish surnames, are asserted to be of the Milesian stem or lineage; as are also the MacDonalds and some others of our Scottish clans. These Milesians are reputed to be the progeny of the sons of Mîl the Gathelian, the king of Galicia in Spain, under those conduct the Gathelians, or Scots, were first brought to and planted in Ireland. So that all surnames in Ireland and Scotland descended from them. They call themselves in their native language *Clann Mîlidh* "the Milesian progeny."[19]

Edmund Burt, *Letters from the North*

Edmund Burt was an English engineer stationed in the Scottish Highlands in the aftermath of the 1715 Jacobite Rising, when the London government decided to create a military infrastructure to occupy and control the Highlands. Burt wrote a series of letters between the 1720s and 1737 to someone in London, providing intelligence about an otherwise poorly understood region. His texts provide a great deal of interesting details about the life of Highlanders at the time, even though he had very limited knowledge of the Gaelic language.

> The Natives (of Inverness) do not call themselves Highlanders, not so much on Account of their low (geographical) Situation, as because they speak English. …

> The Highlanders differ from the people of the low country in almost every circumstance of life. Their language, customs, manners, dress, etc., are unlike, and neither of them would be contented to be taken for the other, insomuch that in speaking of an unknown person of this country (I mean Scotland) as a Scotsman only, it is as indefinite as

barely to call a Frenchman a European, so little would his native character be known by it. ...

The Highlanders are exceedingly proud to be thought an unmixed people, and are apt to upbraid the English with being a composition of all nations ...

They have an adherence one to another, as Highlanders, in opposition to the people of the Low-Country, whom they despise as inferior to them in Courage, and believe they have a right to plunder them whenever it is in their Power. This last arises from a Tradition, that the Lowlands, in old Times were the possessions of their Ancestors.

For notwithstanding the Lowland Scots complain of the English for ridiculing other nations, yet they themselves have a great number of standing jokes upon the Highlanders.[20]

Rev. John Macpherson, *Critical Dissertations*

John Macpherson (1710–1765) studied to be a church minister in Aberdeen and briefly held a position in Barra before he was reassigned to Sleat, Skye, where he later died. His book *Critical Dissertations on the Origin, Antiquities, Language, Government, Manners and Religion of the Antient Caledonians, Their Posterity the Picts, and the British and Irish Scots*, published after he died, defended Gaeldom from the hostility of anglophones scholars critical of the books written by James Macpherson attributed to the poet Ossian.

> The Welsh to this day call the Irish and Scots *Gwyddel*. The Irish and Highlanders of this kingdom give themselves this name reciprocally. ... On the other hand, the English, Welsh, and all who speak English only, are distinguished by the Highlanders and the genuine Irish with the appellation *Gall*. ... formerly an unfavourable idea was annexed to the name of Highlander, and the people of that country, in return, gave the name *Gall* to every foreigner or enemy of their nation, and fixed to it the ideas communicated by the words stranger, ignoble, cowardly, penurious, and inhospitable. ... the genuine Scots call themselves *Gàidheil*, their country *Gàidhealtachd*, and everything that looks like them and their country *Gàidhealach*. ...

> ... the Highlanders of Scotland – they call themselves *Albannaich* to this day. All the illiterate Highlanders are as perfect strangers to the national name of Scot as they are to that of Parthian or Arabian. If a common Highlander is asked of what country he is, he immediately answered that he is an *Albannach* or *Gàidheal*.[21]

Anne Grant, *Essays on the Superstitions*

Anne MacVicar Grant (1755-1838) was born to Highland parents in Glasgow in 1755. In 1779 she married the Rev. James Grant and accompanied him to his Highland parish of Laggan. She was a fluent speaker of both Gaelic and English, and her many letters provide rare and insightful views of Highland life in the eighteenth and early nineteenth centuries. This excerpt is one of first full surviving explanations of the Highland perceptions of Lowlanders.

> No two nations ever were more distinct, or differed more completely from each other, than the highlanders and lowlanders; and the sentiments with which they regarded each other, was at best a kind of smothered animosity.
>
> The lowlander considered the highlander as a fierce and savage depredator, speaking a barbarous language, and inhabiting a gloomy and barren region, which fear and prudence forbid all strangers to explore. The attractions of his social habits, strong attachments, and courteous manners, were confined to his glens and to his kindred. All the pathetic and sublime charms of his poetry, and all the wild wonders of his records, were concealed in a language difficult to acquire, and utterly despised as the jargon of barbarians by their southern neighbours.
>
> If such were the light in which the cultivators of the soil regarded the hunters, graziers, and warriors of the mountains, their contempt was amply repaid by their high spirited neighbours. They again regarded the lowlanders, as a very inferior mongrel race of intruders; sons of little men, without heroism, ancestry, or genius. Mechanical drudges, who could neither sleep upon the snow, compose extempore songs, recite long tales of wonder or of woe, or live without bread and without shelter, for weeks together, following the chase. Whatever was mean or effeminate, whatever was dull, slow, mechanical, or torpid, was in the highlands imputed to the lowlanders, and exemplified by allusions to them; while in the low country, every thing ferocious or unprincipled — every species of aukwardness or ignorance — of pride or of insolence, was imputed to the highlanders.
>
> No two communities, generally speaking, could hate each other more cordially, or despise each other more heartily. Much of this hatred, however, proceeded from ignorance of each other's character and manners.[22]

1 Barrow, "The lost Gàidhealtachd," 74.

2 Boardman and Ross, *The Exercise of Power*, 15-16.

3 Sellar, "Celtic Law," 7; Boardman, "The Campbells," 97.

4 Sellar, "Celtic Law," 5-6; Boardman and Ross, *The Exercise of Power*, 16.

5 Boardman and Ross, *The Exercise of Power*, 18, 19.

6 Foster, "The Topography," 47.

7 Lynch, *Scotland*, 63; Foster, "The Topography," 46.

8 McLeod and Bateman, *Duanaire na Sracaire*, xxv.

9 Dodgshon, *The Age of the Clans*, 16.

10 Gannon, "Ancient DNA."

11 For much more detail about these issues, see Newton, *Warriors of the Word*, 44-79.

12 Clancy, "Scotland, the 'Nennian' recension of the *Historia Brittonum*, and the *Lebor Bretnach*."

13 My translation of Van Hamel, *Lebor Bretnach*, 25-28.

14 Translated and discussed in MacGregor, "Gaelic Barbarity," 7-15.

15 Translation from the website of the National Archives of Scotland, https://webarchive.nrscotland.gov.uk/20170106033856/http://www.nas.gov.uk/downloads/declarationArbroath.pdf

16 Translation (from original Latin) from Constable, *John Major's History*, 48-49, 50.

17 Buchanan, *The History of Scotland*, 43.

18 Brown, *Early Travellers*, 268, 269, 271.

19 Adapted from Buchanan, *Account of the Family of Buchanan*, 158.

20 Simmons, *Burt's Letters*, 19, 153-54, 182, 192, 272.

21 MacPherson, *Critical Dissertations*, 88, 89, 104.

22 Grant, *Essays on the Superstitions*, 27-29.

Chapter Three

What's In A Name?
Personal Names, Clan Names, Emblems

This chapter will enable you to answer the questions:
- What names did Highlanders actually use for themselves?
- What did the term "clan" originally mean and where does it come from?
- What are the real names used for clans and surnames in the Highlands and where do they come from?
- What were the various ways in which Highlanders expressed and recognized their personal and clan identities?

Personal Names

Gaelic society is patriarchal (power is held by men and inherited from fathers) and patrilineal (lineage is understood to pass through father, father's father, etc.), although there are exceptions to this general rule. Even among people descended from Gaels who speak English in Nova Scotia, the first question that one person typically asks the other upon meeting for the first time is, "Who's your father?"

Since the names of kin-groups and clans are based on personal names, we should first discuss the practices for naming individuals as a foundation. If you have done much genealogical research on people in the Highlands, you may have noticed how elusive they can be in officials records or how the names for them seem to change or be inconsistent. This chapter will help to explain why that seems to be the case when looking through the evidence in anglophone documents.

Personal names illustrate how the differences between Gaelic and anglophone societies have become obscured by practices of translation and the assumptions taken by those unaware of the historical complexities of life in the Highlands. While people generally assume that their surname indicates something about the clan affiliation and ancestral territory of their family, "surnames of the present day can be unreliable, and even misleading, as evidence of family origins."[1]

Scottish Highlanders can be known by several different names, depending on who is using the name and the context in which the name is used:

1. First name and/or nickname, used within the family and home community.
2. *Sloinneadh* "patrilineal descent," used among those familiar with the family of origin.
3. First name and surname, used in official records, usually recorded by agents of the state in English and meant for use outside of the home community.

Children were generally given the first name of one of their forebears: according to traditional practice, the first son was named after his grandfather and the second after his father. As a result, a small number of names tend to recur in most families. As George Henderson noted in 1911, "I find with many that it is a matter of extreme importance to call a child by the name of a deceased ancestor." This practice is called *togail an ainm* "raising the name" in Gaelic.[2] There are also traces of other interesting naming practices, as shown in the texts of the Primary Sources section below.

The pool of names used in families and communities tended to be fairly small, certainly much smaller than the total number of people. It is not uncommon for more than one child in a nuclear family to share the same first name. There would usually be multiple people with the same first name within a generation or two of each other within the same extended family. To distinguish between individuals of the same name, adjectives were often added to their first name. In Gaelic, adjectives come after nouns, such as in the famous Highlander *Rob Ruadh* – known in English as "Rob Roy" – whose name translates as "Red-haired Rob."

Adjectives can refer to hair and skin color, the most common of which are below:

Gaelic Term	Meaning	Anglicized As
Bàn	"Blonde, Fair-haired"	Bain, Bane
Ciar	"Swarthy complexion"	Keir
Donn	"Brown-haired, Brunette"	Dunn
Dubh	"Black-haired"	Dow, Dhu

Gaelic Term	Meaning	Anglicized As
Fionn	"Blonde, Fair-haired"	Finn
Glas	"Pale complexion"	
Liath	"Gray-haired"	
Odhar	"Sallow complexion"	Orr, Oure
Riabhach	"Brindled, Streaked brown and grey"	Riach, Reoch, Rayoch
Ruadh	"Red-haired"	Roy

Adjectives can refer to size and relative age, the most common of which are below:

Gaelic Term	Meaning	Anglicized As
Àrd	"Tall"	Aird
Beag	"Small," can also imply "The younger"	Beg
Caol	"Thin"	Kyle
Gearr	"Short"	Gare
Fada	"Long(-legged), Tall"	
Mór	"Big," can also imply "the older"	Mohr, More, Moer
Òg	"Young,, Junior"	
Seann	"Old, The older, Senior"	Shen

Adjectives can refer to distinguishing features or traits, the most common of which are below:

Gaelic Term	Meaning	Anglicized As
Breac	"Pock-marked"	Brek
Cam	"Bent, twisted; Squint'	
Dall	"Blind"	

Gaelic Term	Meaning	Anglicized As
Molach	"Hairy"	

Adjectives can refer to occupations and professions, the most common of which are below:

Gaelic Term	Meaning	Anglicized As
Bard	"(Lower-order) Poet"	Baird
Ceard	"Tin-smith, tinker"	Caird, Card
Gobha	"Smith"	Gow, Gowan
Saor	"Carpenter, Joiner"	
Sagart	"Priest"	Saggart

If some of the above adjectives look familiar, it is likely you have seen them as common elements of nicknames or surnames. If Highland man spawned a successful family, his successors were named after that father for several generations. Once the central government started making records of people in the Highlands and expected them to have family names, one of these elements was often adopted to provide them with a surname.

An important point should be made here about literacy, language, and record keeping. Most all of the documents that we have from the pre-modern period in the Highlands concern high-born families: there was very little need for creating textual records about the peasantry, very few of whom were literate themselves. The central government only started taking an interest in the Highlands at the individual level in the seventeenth century and became more intrusive and demanding in the eighteenth century. It is only at this point that we start to get documents containing the names of tenants on estates in the Highlands. These records were created in English for readers (in Edinburgh or London or other anglophone locations) and relied upon literate intermediaries (such as ministers and estate factors) to create names for people that would be useful for official purposes, but these names are usually inconsistent and often arbitrary. It's not unusual to find the same person given different names in different records, thereby eluding our attempts to track them definitively over time.[3]

One such example is a renowned Gaelic poet who emigrated from Lochalsh in the Highlands to North Carolina and fought as a Loyalist soldier during the American Revolution. In Gaelic he is *Iain mac Mhurchaidh* ("John son of Murdo"), although the use of his clan name would make him *Iain MacRath* ("John MacRae"). Scholars attempting to determine his fate after being captured by American revolutionaries could not find him in the record under these names, and only recently has he been found and recognized under the name "John Murchison." This demonstrates how distorted Gaelic names can become in the anglophone record.

Many people in the Highlands (or in immigrant Gaelic communities) are identified by a nickname (*frith-ainm, far-ainm*, or *leas-ainm*). It is typically a memorable word or phrase referring to a childhood anecdote, a distinguishing characteristic, or an unusual event that replaces the given name of that person for life. It is used most often within a community, but sometimes travels with the individual outside of his home area. *Fionnan MacDhomhnaill*, for example, was a Gael who worked as a fur trader in western Canada. He became known in English as "Big Finan of the Buffalo" because on one expedition he managed to wrestle a buffalo to the ground after a three hour struggle.

The natural way for Gaels to provide a full, identifying name for themselves within their own communities is the *sloinneadh*, a patrilineal line of descent enumerating the names of fathers going back seven or more generations. Icelanders (apart from a small number of immigrant families) also still use this naming system rather than surnames. The word *nighean* means "daughter" but in a *sloinneadh* it usually appears as *nic*.

For example, the first three generations of the *sloinneadh* of the Highland heroine Flora MacDonald are *Fionnaghal nighean Raonuill 'ic Aonghais Òig* ("Flora the daughter of Ronald the son of young Angus"). Notice that her name in her native tongue is not "Flora" at all but *Fionnaghal*, meaning "fair shoulder" and that there is no name like "Donald" in her *sloinneadh*.

Kin-Groups and Terminologies

It is well known that the word "clan" in English is a borrowing from the Gaelic term *clann* meaning "children." It is not as well known that this is just one term that was used to name collective groups of people that had descended from founding fathers in Scotland and Ireland:[4]

Term	Literal Meaning	Usage
cenél	"kindred"	Used by the 6th century, starting to become obsolete in the 10th century
clann	"children"	In use by the 12th century, starting to become obsolete in the 16th century
cinneadh	"kindred"	Starting to replace *clann* in the 16th century

The confusing and chaotic medley of Highland surnames in English hides the logical and consistent system used in Gaelic. In order to understand the origin of these names, you have to understand a little about how clans evolved as social units.

The names used for clans reflect both political power and family genealogy. When a powerful leader had sons, each of his sons would form his own branch on the family tree. Each branch of lineage is called a *sliochd* (singular, *sliochdan* plural) in Gaelic. Eventually, if the leader descended from a particular branch became powerful enough to be a chieftain in his own right, he would be recognized with a title based on the founder of the branch and the people under his governance would be given a *clann* name, usually based on the same founder's first name, to refer to them collectively.

In order to become a successful branch of a clan, the leader and his dependents needed to expand into new territory of their own. The branch and its leader could also be referred to by the territorial name or the place name of the leader's home (the clan's "headquarters").

This can be illustrated by the family history of one of the most successful clans in Scottish history, Clan Donald, which has branches throughout the Highlands. One of the most powerful men in the twelfth century operating around the land we now call Scotland was Somerled (Gaelic *Somhairle*) *mac GilleBride*, who held the title "King of the Hebrides." Although the territory he controlled was split between his three sons, two of his grandsons – *Domhnall* "Donald" and *Ruaidhrí* "Rory" – gained the territory of both their father and uncle. They founded dynasties that were named after them: *Clann Domhnaill* "Clan Donald" (but not "Clan MacDonald," as commonly seen in English nowadays) and *Clann Ruaidhrí*.

The sons of Domhnall – Aonghus and Alastair – would have been called *Aonghuis mac Dhomhnaill* and *Alastair mac Dhomhnaill*, as *mac* means "son" and *Dhomhnaill* is the genitive case of their father's name. Over time, this patrilineal designation was inherited as the surname *MacDhomhnaill* (anglicized as "MacDonald") by the nobility descended from him.

A great many Highland surnames are based on this pattern of *mac* "son" plus personal name (in the genitive case). This should alert us to the fact that the same surnames have emerged for different families from disparate parts of the Highlands. Sharing a surname is no guarantee of a common family origin. A classic example is *MacNéill* (anglicized as "MacNeil," "MacNeal," and so on): one major clan of this name belongs to the island of Gigha in the Inner Hebrides and another belongs to the island of Barra in the Outer Hebrides but they are not directly related.

There is a slew of Highland surnames that have the element *gille* in them. One of the meanings of *gille* is "servant" and it was used by monks who followed a particular saint. Monks were not celibate in medieval Gaeldom and in fact often founded dynasties that monopolized church power, so their devotional titles were inherited by their children. These saint names were sometimes also given to children because they were born on the feast day of a saint.[5] Such names include:

Original Gaelic Surname	Meaning	Anglicized
MacGilleBrìde	"Son of the servant of Bridget"	Gilbride, Gilbert, MacBride
MacGilleChrìosta	"Son of the servant of Christ"	Gilchrist
MacGilleÌosa	"Son of the servant of Jesus"	Gillies, MacLeish
MacGilleFhaolain	"Son of the servant of Faolan"	MacLellan, MacLelland
MacGilleFhinnein	"Son of the servant of Finnan"	MacLennan
MacGilleMhìcheil	"Son of the servant of Michael"	Carmichael
MacGilleMoire	"Son of the servant of Mary"	Gilmore
MacGilleEathain	"Son of the servant of John"	MacLean, MacLane

Not all surnames in the Scottish Highlands, however, follow the *mac* plus first-name pattern. Some surnames of Gaelic origin relate to physical features of the founder of a family. The most prominent of these are *Caimbeul* "Campbell" (meaning "crooked-mouth"), *Camshron* "Cameron" (meaning "crooked nose") and *Ceanaideach* "Kennedy" (originally *Ceann-éitigh* meaning "grim head").

There is also a sizable group of Gaelic surnames that are borrowed or adapted in various ways from French, originally brought by the Anglo-Norman feudal aristocrats. These names include *Cuimein* "Cumming(s)," *Friseal* "Fraser," *Grannd* "Grant," *Siosal* "Chisholm," and *Stiùbhart* "Stewart, Stuart."

Clan Reputations, Rivalries, and Nicknames

Over the long time period in which they were dominant in the Highlands, clan chieftains gained reputations for certain kinds of behavior and characteristics. It is no surprise that they also acquired nicknames that reflect these histories and tendencies, which are also reflected in sayings and explained by historical tales in Gaelic.

A few of these nicknames are alternative surnames based on other legendary figures in the clan lineage. Others offer somewhat wry commentaries or were even used as insults meant to taunt members of the clan. Besides disparaging clans for being poor (accusing them of having only shellfish, porridge, or bad bread to eat), or too sluggish to make their way through the bogs and rough roads in the Highlands (hence keeping their feet clean or white), some clans (especially Campbells, Cummings, and MacPhails) were derided for collaborating with the central government for their own gain against fellow Gaels in the Highlands and hence are accused of being treacherous or crooked-mouthed.

Some of these nicknames are only used in specific districts. It is interesting to see how the same epithets and phrases were applied to different clans in distant areas, reaffirming that Gaels shared similar ways of perceiving actions and allegiances, and common ways of praising and shaming, across the Highlands.

There are typically stories that explain the nicknames and sayings about clans and clan chiefs. The Primary Sources section below contains stories for a selection of these. Here are a few of the more common clan nicknames, ordered by the English form of the clan name:[6]

English Form of Clan Surname	Gaelic Nickname(s)	Meaning
Cameron	Clann Mhaol Onfhaidh	Children of Maol Onfhaidh
	Camshronaich bhog' an ime	The feeble Camerons of the butter (an insult)

English Form of Clan Surname	Gaelic Nickname(s)	Meaning
Campbell	Clann Diarmaid, Clann Duibhne	Children of Diarmaid, Children of Duibhne
	Caimbeulaich nam beul sligneach	Campbells of the scaly mouths
Clark	Cléirich nam beul sleamhainn	Clarks of the slippery mouths
MacCallum	Sliochd nan trì fichead burraidh	Lineage of the sixty fools
MacCodrum	Clann MhicCodruim nan ròn	MacCodrums of the seals
MacGregor	Clann a' cheò	Children of the mist
MacKinnon	Clann Fhionghain nam faochag	MacKinnons of the wilks
MacNicol, Nicholson	MacNeacail a' bhrochain 's an droch arain-eòrna	MacNicol of the porridge and the bad barley bread
MacPherson	Clann Mhuirich a' bhrochain	MacPhersons of the porridge
Martin	Sliochd nan sionnach	Lineage of the foxes
Menzies	Mèinnearaich bhog' a' bhruthaist	The feeble Menzies of the brose
Stewart	Stiùbhartaich nan rìgh 's nan ceàrd	The Stewarts of the kings and tinkers

The reputations and characteristics of clans and clan chiefs, as well as rivalries between them, are also reflected in a number of proverbs and sayings in Gaelic (see further details for some of these in the Primary Sources section below). Most of the longer sayings as structured as poetic couplets with internal rhymes.

Clan	Saying	Translation and Meaning
Cameron	Iarr gach nì air Camshronach ach na iarr ìm air.	Ask a Cameron for anything but butter.
Campbell	Fhad 's a bhios maide 's a' choille, cha bhi Caimbeulach gun fhoill.	For as long as there is a stick in the forest, there won't be a Campbell without treachery.

Clan	Saying	Translation and Meaning
Cumming	Fhad 's a bhios maide 's a' choille, bidh foille 's na Cuimeinich.	For as long as there is a stick in the forest, the Cummings will be treacherous.
Grants	Cha bhi gean air Granndach gus am faigh e an lite.	A Grant is in a foul mood until he gets his porridge.
Kennedy	Tha 'fhortan fhéin air MacUalraig, biodh e cruaidh no biodh e bog.	Kennedy will have his own luck, be it hard or be it soft.
MacArthur	MacArtuir Shrath Churra. o bhun an stuic fheàrna.	MacArthur of Strachur, from the root of the alder.
	Cnuic is sluic is Ailpeinich ach cuin a thàinig Arturaich?	Hills, hollows, and MacAlpines, but when did the MacArthurs arrive?
	Maorach Cailleach MhicArtuir: partan is dà fhaochaig.	The shell-fish of old lady MacArthur: a crab and two whelks.
MacDiarmid	Clann Diarmaid nam busa dubha, cuiribh riutha 's beiribh orra.	MacDiarmids of the black mouths, go at them and catch them.
MacDonald	Faram is na toiream, fasan Chlann Domhnaill.	Give to me but I don't give, Clan Donald's fashion.
	Sann an deireadh an latha is fhearr na Domhnallaich.	The MacDonalds are best at the end of the day.
	B' fhearr do MhacDhomhnaill comhdach a bhith aige dha fhéin.	MacDonald prefers to have his own shelter for himself.
MacDonald and MacLean	Spagadagliog Chlann Domhnaill is leòm Leathanaich.	MacDonald swagger and MacLean pretense.
MacGregor and MacNab	Cha robh balach riamh de Chloinn Ghriogair no caile de Chloinn an Aba.	The MacGregors never had a loutish boy nor the MacNabs a strumpet of a girl.
Macintosh	Chan ann a h-uile latha a bhios mòd aig Mac an Tòisich.	It's not every day that Macintosh holds court.
	Fadal Chlann an Tòisich.	The tardiness of the Macintoshes.

Clan	Saying	Translation and Meaning
	Casan tioram Chlann an Tòisich.	Dry-footed Macintoshes.
Macintyre	Clann an t-Saoir gheala-chas.	Clean-footed Macintyres.
	Craobh de dh'abhall a' ghàrraidh aig taobh Loch Éite agus Mac an t-Saoir Ghlinn Nodha, dà thuathanach as sine an Albainn.	An apple tree on Loch Etive-side and Macintyre of Glennoe, the two most ancient cultivators in Scotland.
MacKay	A h-uile fear a théid a dholaidh, gheibh e dolar o MacAoidh.	Every man who goes broke will get a dollar from MacKay.
	Ma tha mise truagh, se mo thruaighe MacAoidh.	If I am in bad shape, I feel worse for MacKay.
MacKenzie	Cha bhi gean air Cloinn Choinnich gus am faigh iad an diathad.	MacKenzies are in a foul mood until they get their meal.
	Fhad 's a bhios monadh an Ceann-Tàile, cha bhi MacCoinnich gun àl 's a' chrò.	For as long as there is moor in Kintail, MacKenzie will have cattle in the fold.
MacKillop	Amhlaireachd Chlann Mhic Fhilip.	The absurd play of the MacKillops.
MacLean	Ged tha mi bochd, tha mi uasal; buidheachas do Dhia, is ann do Chloinn GhillEathain mi.	Although I am poor, I am noble; thanks to God I belong to the MacLeans.
	An cinneadh mór, is am pòr mì-shealbhach.	The great clan, although the seed is unfortunate.
	Mar mhadadh ag òl eanraich, tha ainmean Chlann Ghilleathain: Eachann, Lachann, Eachann, Lachann...	MacLean names sound like a hound slurping soup: Eachann, Lachann, Eachann, Lachann ...
	MacGilleathain Locha Buidhe, ceann-uidhe nam mèirleach.	MacLean of Lochbuy, destination of thieves.
MacLean, Clanranald	An t-uasal Leathanach 's an ceatharnach Raghnallach.	The noble MacLean and the warrior Clanranald.

Clan	Saying	Translation and Meaning
MacLeans, MacDonalds, Campbells	Leathanach gun bhòst, Domhnallach gun tapadh, Caimbeulach gun mhòrchùis: trì rudan ainneamh.	A humble MacLean, a listless MacDonald, a non-pompous Campbell: three rare things.
MacNeil	Chan ann a h-uile latha a théid MacNéill air each.	It's not every day that MacNeil mounts his horse.
MacNicol, Nicholson	Far am bi fidheall no pìob, bidh MacNeacail.	MacNicol will be wherever there is a fiddle or bagpipe.
MacPhail	Fhad 's a bhios fuachd ann an stoc-càil, bidh an fhoill ann an Cloinn Phàil.	For as long as the kail-runt is cold, the MacPhails will be treacherous.
Matheson	Có dha bhios MacMhathain gu math mur bi dha fhéin?	Who should Matheson treat well if not himself?

Clans, Tartans and Badges

One of the first things that people typically hear about clans is that each clan has its own tartan that provides a visual marker for their identity. Although tartans provide beautiful patterns of colors that hold meaning for people today, the idea that every clan has its own tartan has no basis in the history of the Highland clan system but was invented in the mid-nineteenth century – well after the collapse of Gaelic society – in order to sell heritage merchandise to urbanites who had become uprooted from their rural roots.

What clan members did actually wear to identify themselves in previous eras when they went into battle was leaves and sprigs of plants. This badge was sometimes placed on top of a pole or else worn in the bonnet of a warrior for individual identification.

What principles led a clan to choose a particular badge? They would first of all be limited by the plants readily available within their natural environment during most of the year. Among those available, the choice might make some symbolic statement relating to the landscape of their homeland, make a play on words (based on the Gaelic names for the plant, their clan, or their land), recall a tale of their ancestors, or use foliage as a magical charm against harm during warfare. There seems to be examples of all of these in the choice of a clan badge.

It's no longer possible to gather a complete list, but there is direct evidence of the following plant badges in reliable sources:

Clan	Tree or Plant Badge
Cameron	*Darach* "Oak"
Campbell	*Roid* "Bog-myrtle"
Clan Chattan	*Giuthas* "Scots Pine"
Fraser	*Iubhar* "Yew"
MacDonald	*Fraoch* "Heather"
MacGregor	*Giuthas* "Scots Pine"
MacKinnon	*Achlasan Chaluim Cille* "St. John's wort"
Menzies	*Fraoch* "Heather"
Robertson	*Raithneach* "Bracken"

What of Clan Septs?

If you go to clan booths at Highland Games, you will likely see a chart which claims that if you have a particular surname, then you are a sept of their clan. Although this is not a complete fabrication, it is a vast simplification of the very complex and fluid operation of clans in the Highlands, who were constantly adding and losing families (who did not even use surnames) over time. Whether or not it is intentional, this claim reinforces the fiction that clans were static kin-groups fixed by ancestry rather than being dynamic social groups constantly adapting to changing circumstances.

In reality, people could easily transfer their loyalty to a different clan chief in order to become his clients and enjoy his protection, especially if they could offer him services that he needed, like occupying and defending land. It was typical for such families to take the chieftain's surname as their own surname, if one was called for.

Evidence that a person or family of a particular surname, at one time or another, lived on the estate of a clan chief or accepted his overlordship was used in the nineteenth century to create simplistic charts assigning surnames to clans. These charts should not fool us into believing that all families with a specific surname were descended from or permanently attached to a particular clan or chieftain. If septs were a social reality in the Highland clan system, there would be a term in Gaelic for them, but there is not.

There are several Gaelic sayings that reflect the change of a surname on the basis of pledging loyalty to a new clan chief. The Gaelic saying *Frisealaich boll na mine* "Frasers of the boll of grain," which circulated around Beauly (in the central Highlands), was applied to people whose surname was originally Bisset but who, in dire straits, accepted the overlordship of the Frasers. A similar saying in the central Highlands was *Cuimeinich clach nan cearc* "The Cummings of the hen stone." This referred to people from neighboring districts (including Farquharsons, Forbeses, Gordons, and Grants) who had taken the surname *Cuimein* "Cumming" because of needing the protection of *Gioban Mór Cuimeineach* "Big Gilbert Cumming." He bestowed his surname on adopted clan members through a re-baptism ritual in which he used water from a stone trough for hens which stood by the door of his castle.[7]

Many people outside of Scotland engage in Highland heritage through clan organizations, but the narrow kin-based focus of these groups has the unfortunate effect of fragmenting Gaelic identity and culture into arbitrary factions that would have been temporary in most cases. Highlanders shared a common Gaelic culture that united them, moving between clan allegiances and affiliations according to shifts of power and fortune. Regardless of this, they had an overarching Gaelic identity and this was more fundamental to their sense of self than the kin-group to which they happened to be associated at any particular time.

Primary Sources

Edmund Burt, *Letters from the North*

In this letter, Burt explains the Gaelic naming system to his reader in England in a surprisingly useful and accurate way.

> The different surnames of the Highlanders in general are but few, in regard they are divided into large families, and hardly any male strangers have intermarried with or settled among them; and with respect to particular tribes, they commonly make that alliance among themselves, who are all of one name, except some few, who may have

affected to annex themselves to the clan, and those, for the most part, assume the name (without giving up their own).

Thus the surnames, being useless for distinction of persons, are suppressed, and there remain only the Christian names; of which there are everywhere a great number of Duncans, Donalds, Alexanders, Patricks, &c. who, therefore, must be some other way distinguished one from another. This is done by some additional names and descriptions taken from their forefathers; for when their own Christian name, with their father's name and description (which is for the most part the colour of the hair), is not sufficient, they add the grandfather's, and so upwards, till they are perfectly distinguished from all others of the same clan-name. As, for example, a man whose name is Donald Grant, has for patronymic (as they call it) the name following, viz.

Domhnall Bàn	i.e., Fair-haired Donald
mac Dhomhnaill Bhàin	Son of fair-haired Donald
mhic Dhomhnaill Ruaidh	Son of red-haired Donald
mhic Iain	Son of John

Thus, you see, the name of Grant is not used, because all of that clan are either so called, or assume that name.

Another thing is, that if this man had descended in a direct line, as eldest, from John, the remotest ancestor, and John had been a chief, he would only be called *MacIain*, leaving out all the intermediate successions by way of eminence.

These patronymical names, at length, are made use of chiefly in writings, receipts, rentals, &c. and, in ordinary matters, the Highlanders have sometimes other distinctions, which also to some are pretty long.

When numbers of them, composed from different tribes, have been jointly employed in a work, they have had arbitrary and temporary denominations added to their Christian names by their overseers, for the more ready distinction; such as the place they came from, the person who recommended them, some particular vice, or from something remarkable in their persons, &c. by which fictitious names they have also been set down in the books of their employers.[8]

Alexander Nicolson, *Gaelic Proverbs*

Donald Macintosh, a native of Highland Perthshire, published the first collection of Gaelic proverbs and idiomatic expressions in 1785. Alexander Nicolson of Skye published a greatly expanded version of this collection in

1881. Although Gaelic sayings about clans are evocative, they can also be obtuse and confusing without the stories that explain them.

An t-uasal Leathaineach, 's an ceatharnach Raonallach.
The gentleman of Clan MacLean, and the warrior of Clanranald.

The MacLeans have generally got credit for a certain high-bred polish, on which they rather plume themselves.' *An cinne mór, 's am pòr mìshealbhach* — "The great race, and the unfortunate seed," is one of their sayings of themselves. Another is, *Ged tha mi bochd, tha mi uasal, — buidheachas do Dhia, 's ann de Chlann Illeathain mi!* — "Though I am poor, I am well-born — God be thanked, I am a MacLean!" The Macdonalds, on the other hand, bear the character of manliness and force, with a tendency to swagger. *Spagadagliog Chlann Domhnaill agus leòm Leathaineach.* — "The Macdonald ostentation, and the MacLean affection," is a saying of this import.

Camshronaich bhog' an ime.
The soft buttery Camerons.

This, like most similar sayings about clans, originated, of course, among enemies. The Camerons were said to be very fond of butter; but who could deny that they were brave?

Chan ann a h-uile latha bhios mòd aig Mac an Tòisich.
It is not every day that Macintosh holds a court.

Toschach or Macintosh of Monyvaird, chamberlain to the Earl of Perth, held a regality court at Monyvaird: it is commonly reported that he caused one to be hanged each court day, in order to make himself famous, and to strike terror into the thieves, which severity occasioned the above saying.

Chan ann a h-uile latha théid Mac Néill air 'each.
It is not every day that MacNeill mounts his horse.

This refers to MacNeill of Barra, whose rocky island territory was more suited for boating than for riding.

Cha bhi gean air Granndaich gus am faigh iad lite.
Grants are not gracious till they get their porridge.

This is merely an alliterative version of the general observation, that a man is not in such good humour before meat as after it. The same thing is said of the Campbells, the Gunns, and the MacKenzies, substituting *diota* or *biadh* for *lite*.

Cho fad 's a bhios craobh 's a' choill, bidh foill anns a' Chuimeanach.

As long as trees are in the wood, the Cumming will be treacherous.

This is one out of several similar sayings, which, it is hoped, will give no offence now to any members of the clans so characterized. The Cumming one is selected as a leading specimen, because it is perhaps the oldest, having probably originated in the time of King Robert the Bruce, who punished the treachery of his cousin the Red Cumyn in such a memorable way at Dumfries.

Cho fad 's a bhios slat an coill', bidh foill ann an Caimbeulach.

bestows the same character on the great Campbell clan, a saying probably dating from the massacre of Glencoe.

Cho fad 's a bhios maid' an coill, cha bhi Mathanach gun fhoill.

euphoniously proclaims the same of the respectable tribe of Matheson. The Munros are similarly libelled. More stiffly, and with as little known reason, it is said of the MacPhails,

Fhad 's a bhios fuachd ann an stoc càil, bidh an fhoill ann an Cloinn Phàil.
While there's cold in stock of kail, there will be guile in a Mac Phail.

Cho fad 's a bhios monadh an Cinn t-sàile, cha bhi MacCoinnich gun àl 's a' chrò.
As long as there are moors in Kintail, Mackenzie won't want cattle in the pen.

This referred to the ancient lords of Kintail, the last of whom died in 1815. The word *crò* has a double meaning here, being the name of a part of Kintail, so called from the river Croe.

Rev. John G. Campbell, *Clan Traditions and Popular Tales*

This description of a Highland naming practice – uncommon in recent times – is drawn from a folktale collected by the Reverend John G. Campbell, probably on the island of Tiree in the 1860s.

His first name is somewhat peculiar, and not common among the MacLeans or any other West Highland clan, and was given to him in this manner. The heir of Torloisk was a promising healthy boy, but the succeeding children of the then chief were dying young. The Chief was then advised by the sages of his race to give to his child the name of the first person whom he met on the way to have the child baptized. The first person encountered was a poor beggar man who had the name of Maol Ìosa "Servant of Jesus." A name given in this way was known as *ainm-rathaid*, or road-name, and was deemed as proof against evil.[9]

William MacKenzie, *The Book of Arran*

This collection of Gaelic folklore recorded on the isle of Arran in the late nineteenth century contains a wealth of information about Highland tradition in the everyday life of people and is an excellent example of early ethnography. The excerpts below relate in various ways to names and naming practices, including clan nicknames and the animals associated with clans that helped to interpret the meaning of dreams.

> It is alleged (in Arran) to have been an ancient Highland custom, before surnames, to call a child by the name of the first thing which attracted the notice of the baptismal party on their way to church. This is said to explain the cuckoo (in the name of a local family). Another name of the type is MacOnie ("son of the rabbit"). …
>
> Up to twenty or thirty years ago, in Arran, if people dreamt of certain animals or birds they were said to have dreamt of certain families or clans. For instance, a young woman named MacAlister reported one morning that during the previous night she dreamt that while walking across the Mòine Mór she was followed by a dog, which jumped on her at last and completely swallowed her. Her mother laughingly replied that it was evident she was not destined to change her name when she married, for a MacAlister would carry her off. Possibly the mother had a shrewd idea where her daughter's affections lay, as the latter did marry a MacAlister. The parties lived about one hundred years ago.
>
> A certain person once reported that he had dreamt he was watching with great interest the flight of a flock of pigeons, which finally landed on a certain field and appeared to consider themselves at home. The explanation that was given for the pigeons coming to stay was that the land on which they had alighted would pass into possession of the MacKelvies.
>
> On one occasion a woman of the name of Currie and a woman of the MacGregors got into an argument which finally waxed somewhat hot, the locality being Lag na Mòine (Shisken), a place where some families named Currie had at one time held farms which had passed into the possession of MacGregors, the Curries viewing the instalment of their successors with rather bitter feelings.
>
> The Currie woman finally made a slighting allusion to the reasons for the MacGregors coming to Arran, many having come for sanctuary when the clan was outlawed and hunted like wild beasts from their native straths. *'Dé thug na coin-dhubha dh'Arainn?'* ("What brought the

blood-hounds to Arran?"). Quick as a flash came the retort of the MacGregor woman: '*Thàinig iad a ruagadh nam feadagan á Lag na Mòine*' ("They came to hunt the plovers out of Lag na Mòine").

The *riochd* of a Macgregor was the bloodhound, that of a Currie the plover.

<u>*Riochd nan Daoine*: Dream Signs of the People</u>

  MacGregors: bloodhounds
  MacAlisters: sheep dogs
  Curries: plovers
  MacNicols: cats
  Hamiltons: hares
  MacLardys: asses
  Bannantynes: mice
  Robertsons: rats
  Stewarts: lions
  MacKinnons: rabbits
  Sillars: frogs
  MacKelvies: doves
  MacDonalds: sheep dogs
  MacKenzies: bees
  Cooks: pigs, bulls
  Kerrs: sheep
  MacNeils: dun bull
  MacMillans: wood-pigeons
  Fullartons: geese
  MacMasters: pigs
  MacNeishes: cats[10]

T. D. MacDonald, *Gaelic Proverbs*

In this collection of Gaelic proverbs and idiomatic expressions, T. D. MacDonald provides an important explanation of the meaning of a saying associated with the chieftain of the MacKays.

A h-uile fear a théid a dholaidh, gheibh e dolar bho MhacAoidh.
Every man who's down in luck, will get a dollar from MacKay.

Said when the Chief of the Mackays was raising men to fight in the wars of Gustavus Adolphus, where he and they made themselves famous. The saying shows that the derogatory attitude of the community towards army rankers is of older growth than is generally supposed. Within our own times soldiering has become quite respectable from the social point of view, but not so long ago it was considered the harbour for all ne'er-do-weels.[11]

Anonymous, "Clan Nick-Names"

There are many rhymes in Gaelic that describe the inhabitants of districts, sometimes associating them with particular emblematic animals. Since a specific district tended to be dominated by a particular clan, this suggests a system of heraldic or totemic animals, defined at a local rather than national scale.

Glassary was (the home of Clan Iver) and there is a piece of Gaelic folk-lore which associates the horse with the MacIvers, just as the magpie was considered friendly to the Campbells, *gille-ruith-nan-Caimbeulach* "the Campbells' messenger" :–

Crodh maol Chnapadail
Eich chloimheach Ghlas Àirigh
Fithich dhubha Chreig Innis
Is coilich Àirigh Sgeòd Innis.

The polled cattle of Knapdale
The shaggy horses of Glassary
The black ravens of Craignish
And the cocks of Ariskedonish.[12]

---

[1] Matheson, *Highland Surnames*, 3.

[2] Henderson, *Survivals in Belief*, 19.

[3] Matheson, *Highland Surnames*, 3-5; Dodgshon, *From Chiefs to Landlords*, 41-50.

[4] Bannerman, "The Scots Language," 5-6.

[5] Black, *The Surnames of Scotland*, xxxvii.

[6] I have amalgamated a number of sources here, particularly *The Highlander* August 1881, 54-55; *The Celtic Monthly* 19 (1911), 67, 113; Nicolson, *Gaelic Proverbs*; MacDonald, *Gaelic Proverbs*, 149-156.

[7] Mitchell, "Vacation Notes," 672; Black, *Surnames*, xxxviii.

[8] Simmons, *Burt's Letters*, 198-99. I have corrected the Gaelic.

[9] Campbell, *Clan Traditions*, 29.

[10] MacKenzie, *Book of Arran*, vol. 2, 118, 289-90.

[11] MacDonald, *Gaelic Proverbs*, 150.
[12] *The Celtic Monthly* 24 (1917), 112.

Chapter Four

As Old As The Mist
Origin Legends

This chapter will enable you to answer the questions:.
- What kinds of stories did Highlanders tell to explain the origins of clans?
- What were the purposes that these origins legends served at the times that they were created and told?
- How can these origin legends be most productively read and understood by us today?

He Who Controls the Past…

It is natural for the power of institutions and political leaders to be backed up by persuasive stories that validate their legitimacy. Stories evolved over time that explained the origins of Highland clans, and while many contain historical facts, we should not read them expecting them to be realistic historical accounts in the same sense as those written by trained historians today. We should rather see them as persuasive stories created to address to the concerns of the times in which they were told.

In the introduction to his account of the Campbells of Craignish (written in about the year 1720), Alasdair Campbell explained that he wrote it to satisfy his curiosity about the origins of his family but also to influence the way that others would interpret the story of this powerful clan in later times:

> It is natural for all men to have a bias or propensity chiefly to that which most nearly concerns themselves, and must own the same if they confess the truth. So I frankly acknowledge that my first desire to look into the abstruse secrets of antiquity was principally founded on the desire I had of setting the story of this branch of which I myself am a son in a true light, being a debt I think I indispensably owe to posterity.[1]

Only the largest and most powerful clans had official histories written for them in early times, but hardly anything that was written before the seventeenth century has survived. The Highlands were being drawn into British and international politics at that time, and the means by which political power was legitimated, negotiated, and asserted was changing. Clan leaders wanted to raise the perceived status and authority of their families, and the writing of clan histories served a number of purposes to them, such as the legitimacy of a particular line of descent.

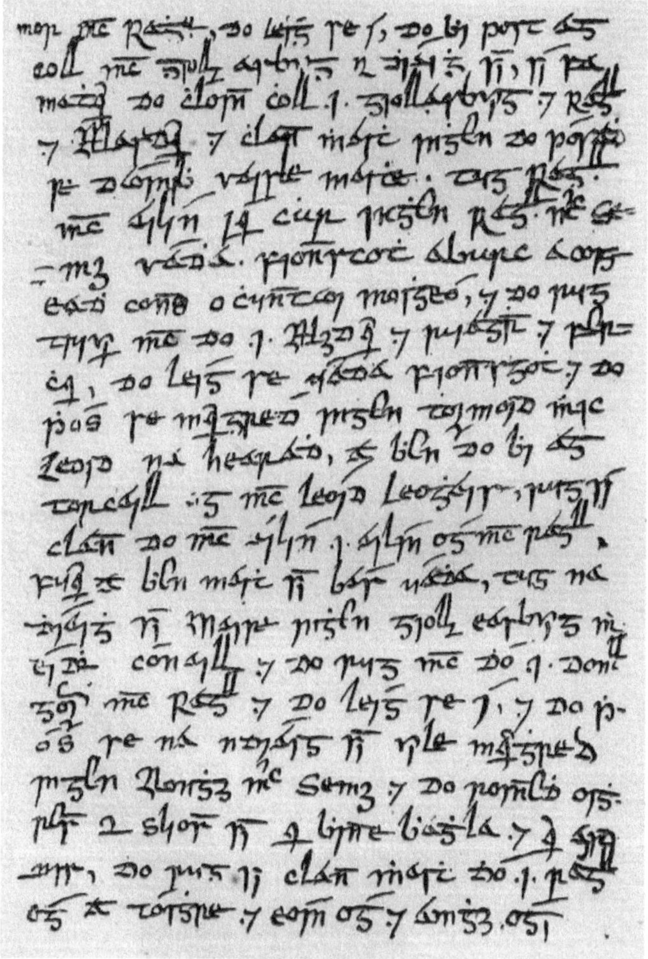

Figure 4.1: A page from the Red Book of Clanranald

Origin legends about Highland clans tend to:
• provide a lineage for the founder of the clan that would be seen as being among people of high social status
• demonstrate that the founder of the clan had the qualities expected of a strong leader

- make symbolic statements about the clan's dynastic or ethnic allegiances within Scotland
- legitimate the occupation of the lands of the clan
- reinforce the connections to and loyalty of lateral branches of the clan
- contain dramatic episodes that make for enjoyable and memorable literature

Arguably the most important of the surviving clan histories is the Red Book of Clanranald, written by the *seanchaidh* Niall MacMhuirich in about the year 1686. This is the only account that was written entirely in Gaelic and it draws upon even earlier texts by the professional literati employed by the Clan Donald Lords of the Isles.

Most of the surviving written versions of clan origin legends were written down between the mid-seventeenth and mid-nineteenth centuries, well past the time that they portray.[2] Oral traditions circulating among Gaelic speakers starting to be transcribed in the mid-nineteenth century, with accounts recorded by folklorists into the mid-twentieth century. Many of these "clan sagas" (as John MacInnes calls them) contain dramatic episodes told with a finely-tuned literary flair.

There are some common motifs in these origin legends: the founders usually come from the pan-Gaelic world of Ireland and Scotland, although the rising tide of English domination motivated some writers to invent French-Norman ancestry; the most common foes are the Norse, portrayed as hostile invaders; clan founders often flee from their original home to a new land and are accepted because of demonstrating their worthiness.

Several of the tales about clan leaders that survived in Gaelic oral tradition among the Highland peasantry in the nineteenth century focus on the use of written charters to assert land rights. This seems to reflect the anxiety of the general population in the Highlands, given the power invested in these documents and the capriciousness of those empowered to use them. The tale below about MacDonalds taking over the Livingston lands of Dalness is one such example.

Primary Sources

The Origin of the MacDonalds

This extract of the origin legend of Clan Donald is adapted from a translation from the Red Book of Clanranald, written by *seanchaidh* Niall MacMhuirich in about 1686. Although historians now believe that

Somerled (called *Somhairle* in Gaelic) had mixed Gaelic-Norse ancestry, the Clan Donald origin legend made him into a champion of the Gaelic cause, fighting off the incursion of unwanted Norse invaders. It is also important to understand that Tara was the symbolic capital of Ireland and carried the symbolic weight of Gaelic authority, so a message about the succession of leadership from Tara would have carried similar import to an election held in Rome for a new Pope.

GilleBrìde was living among his kin in Ireland, the MacGuires and MacMathons. These groups held an assembly on the estate of MacGuire in Fermanagh and among their discussions, they decided that GilleBrìde should regain some of his ancestral territory, since he had been exiled from it by the power of the Norse.

When GilleBrìde saw a large group of stout young men in the assembly who were supportive of him, he asked a favor of his kin, that as many men as the fort next to them could hold be allowed to go with him to Scotland in order that he recapture his rightful patrimony.

GilleBrìde proceeded with the host to Scotland and landed there. They made frequent attacks on their enemies during this conflict, for their enemies were numerous and powerful. All of the islands from Man to Orkney, and all of the coastline from Dumbarton to Caithness, were in the possession of the Norse; and the Gaels of those lands who survived were defending themselves in the mountains and forests. And toward the end of that time, GilleBrìde had a good son, who came of age and was renowned.

It happened that the small army who were followers of GilleBrìde and Somerled were in the forests and mountains of Ardgour and Morvern, and a large army of Norsemen attacked them by surprise. Somerled gathered the soldiers and raiding parties around him and arranged them in front and rear. Somerled put them in battle order and made a great display of them to his enemies. He marched them three times in front of the enemy, so that they were given the impression that these were three different groups.

After that, they attacked and Somerled and his army defeated his enemies. He did not stop pursuing them until he drove them northward across the river Sheil, and some of them escaped with their king to the islands. And he did not stop that work until he cleared the Norse out of the western part of Scotland – except from the Outer Hebrides – gaining victory over his enemies in every field of battle.

Somerled spent his time alternately in peace and war until he marched with an army to the region of Glasgow when he was assassinated in 1164 by his own page, who took his head to the King of Scotland. His own people assert that he did not make that expedition to make war against the King but to seek peace, for he did more to conquer the King's enemies than to bring conflict to him.

Somerled had a good family, his sons Dougall, Ranald and MacSgillinn, and his daughter Beathag. Beathag was a religious woman and nun who founded the Church of Cairinis in Uist. Dougall, son of Somerled, took over the leadership of Argyll and Lorne. Ranald and his progeny went to the Hebrides and Kintyre, and his sons succeeded him.

Ranald, King of the Hebrides and Argyll, was the most distinguished of the Gaelicized Norse for prosperity, generosity, and battle feats. He founded three monasteries: two in Iona and one in Kintyre. Let it be known that Ranald and his army were the greatest power that King Alexander of Scotland had against the King of Norway. ...

Messages came from Tara that Donald, son of Ranald, should take over the leadership of the Hebrides and the greater territory of the Gaels. He had good children ...[3]

The Origin of the MacKenzies

The following extract from the history of the MacKenzies was written by Iain ("John") Molach MacKenzie of Applecross in about the year 1667. The MacKenzies came to act as agents of the central government in the Highlands, and this position as intermediary power brokers helps to explain why they created an ancestral link to the Anglo-Normans in their origin story and why they are portrayed as attracting the envy and suspicion of the natives where they went.

Colin Gerald, with his brother GilleEathain Gerald, came to Scotland in the reign of King Alexander III when King Alexander was vanquishing the Norse from the possession of the Isles of Scotland. This Colin was one of the five sons of Maurice FitzGerald, Lord Justice of Ireland and Earl of Desmond who was made Lord Justice of Ireland in the year of our savior 1228 and continued so with great praise of his valor and wit in managing the troublesome affairs of Ireland until the year 1249 when King Henry III removed him upon misinformation of those who envied his place.

This noble family of the Geraldines was of the nobility of Florence, came thence to Normandy and came from Normandy with William the Conqueror to England ...

Now I am to speak of Colin Gerald and his successors in Scotland since their coming to Scotland to Alexander III in the year 1260 when he and his brother GilleEathain did serve. They were with him at the Battle of Largs in Cunningham and followed him in all the wars with the Norse until King Alexander came to drive the Norse from their possessions in the Isles in which voyage he built Eilean Donnain. This house he did build to be a stronghold over the islanders, which he gave to be commanded to Colin Gerald, honoring him with the honor of knighthood, called him "Sir Colin." He also gave him the lands of Lagan Achadh an Droma as a testimony of his good service. ...

Colin Gerald named his son *Coinneach* ("Kenneth") after his grandfather. He was the second of that family who was Lord of Kintail and after him, his whole family was called *MacCoinnich* ("MacKenzie"). ...[4]

The Origin of the Macintyres

This origin legend of the Macintyres is embedded in a history of the Clan Donald which was probably written by Ùisdean MacDonald of North Uist between 1660 and 1685.[5] Versions of this origin legend have survived in Gaelic oral tradition to the present day.

Olaf the Red, King of the Isle of Man, Islay, Mull, and the Inner Hebrides, came with his fleet to Loch Stornua in order to subdue all of the Hebrides, south and north, pretending to have his rule from the King of Denmark, to whom the older settlement of Norsemen north of Ardnamurchan refused allegiance.

As Olaf encamped at Loch Stornua, Somerled came to the other side of the loch and cried out, "If Olaf is there, how did he fare?"

Olaf replied that he was well.

"Then," said Somerled, "I come from Somerled, Thane of Argyll, who promises to assist you in your expedition on the condition that you bestow you daughter on him."

Olaf responded that he knew that it was Somerled himself who was speaking and that he would not give up his daughter, but that he and his men should follow him on the expedition. So Somerled resolved to follow Olaf.

At that time one of Olaf's company was one of his foster-brothers, a man named Muiris MacNéill, and he was Somerled's close friend. When Somerled brought his two galleys near the place where Olaf left his ship, thus Muiris came to where Somerled was and said that he would find a means by which he might come to get Olaf's daughter. So, in the night time, he bored Olaf's ship under water with many holes and made a pin for each hole, filling them with tallow and butter.

When they got up in the morning and set out to sea, after passing the point of Ardnamurchan, Olaf's ship sprang a leak: the ship tossing on the waves cast the tallow and butter out of the holes and it was beginning to sink. Olaf and his men cried out to Somerled for help.

Muiris replied that Somerled would not save him unless he bestowed his daughter on him. At last, Olaf, being in danger of his life, confirmed by oath that he would give his daughter to Somerled, who received him immediately in his galley. Muiris went into Olaf's galley and fixed the pins in the holes which he had formerly prepared for them and by this means they landed in safety.

From that time to this day the posterity of Muiris are called *Mac an t-Saoir* (Macintyre, "The Son of the Carpenter").[6]

The Origin of the Campbells

The Rev. Robert Duncansone, minister of Campbelltown, wrote this history of the Campbells some time between 1670 and 1676, although he claimed he was "assisted by several other good *seanchaidh*s" and the Earl of Argyll.[7] This exercise in historical creativity reflects the efforts of the Campbells to maximize their reach into multiple political and cultural realms by claiming a multitude of ethnic lineages for themselves: they connect themselves to the Fenian hero Diarmad (thus giving themselves bona fide Gaelic credentials), they profess a stake in Arthurian legend (and thus in the pre-Anglo-Saxon antiquity of the island of Britain), and they extend the adventures of their ancestors to Normandy in France (so as to include the ascendant dominance of the Anglo-Normans).

An account of the genealogy of the Campbells who were of old called *Clann Ó Duibhne*. I say of old, so called from the famous knights and champions of the Ó Duibhne, and especially from Diarmad Ó Duibhne, famous in the Irish genealogies, from whom they are sometimes designated *Sìol Diarmaid* "the Seed of Diarmaid" or *Sliochd Dhiarmaid* "the lineage of Diarmaid," but assumed the surname of Campbells in the days of Malcolm III, otherwise called Malcolm

Ceannmór, King of Scotland, who nevertheless keep the names both of Campbells and Ó Duibhne to this day. ...

The name of Campbell both in the Highlands and Lowlands of Scotland, and particularly their Chief, under the name of The Knight of Lochow, before they were made noble, are mentioned as famous for their faithfulness to the Crown and Kingdom in the history of Sir William Wallace and of King Robert of Bruce about 350 or 360 years ago, as also in the beginning of the reign of the Stewarts ...

Although the common and ordinary account of the genealogy of the name of Campbell or Clann Ó Duibhne commences from Arthur of the Round Table, King of the Britons, as a very famous and great person, yet we will commence it some ages before him by showing you the occasion of his coming to the Crown of the Britons ...

Smeirbhidh Mór, son of Arthur, was a great and famous person of whom diverse and strange things are spoken in Gaelic tradition; it is said that he was born in Dumbarton on the south side, in a place called an *Tùr an Talla Dheirg* ("The Tower of the Red Hall"). He was called by his byname "The Foot of the Forest" because he was a wild, undaunted person. He was married to a sister of King Aedán of Scotland, who was a good, virtuous and pious king, being contemporaneous with Saint Colm Cille ("Columba"), who founded Iona. ...

Smeirbhidh Mór married a daughter of the Duke of Valencia and they begat Duibhne Mór, from whom the Clann Ó Duibhne are named. ...

Diarmaid Ó Duibhne (from whom the Campbells are called *Sìol Dhiarmaid*) was a great and eminent person in Ireland and very honorably mentioned in the Irish traditional antiquities as a person of great courage and strength, and very amiable to be looked upon. He had as his wife Gràinne, daughter of Cormac mac Airt mhic Chuinn Cheudchathaich, whereby the Campbells are descended of the noble race of the O'Neills. ...

and he had a son called Duibhne Deudgheal ("White-Toothed"), who had a son GilleChaluim, who went to Normandy in France and took in marriage the heiress of Beauchamps – that is to say, *Campus Bellus*, or "Pleasant Field" – being the daughter of the sister of William the Conqueror.[8]

The Origin of the MacRaes / MacRaths

The Reverend John MacRa graduated from the University of Aberdeen in 1667 and died in 1704. The following is an extract from his history of the MacRaes, written sometime between those two dates. He attempts to explain the meaning of the surname by recounting a story in which an heroic utterance in battle becomes a nickname that sticks to his descendants. This is a common literary device in Gaelic tradition that should not be taken as literal truth. MacRa is one of the first writers to observe that some Highlanders removed the Gaelic element *mac* "son" from their surname when they migrated to anglophone regions due to anti-Gaelic prejudices.

> As to the origin of the MacRas, tradition tells us of a desperate conflict between the princes of two tribes in Ireland. A certain young man signified himself by his prowess, defending himself from an attack of his enemy. As people observed their combat, he said in Gaelic that he was *duine ratha* "a fortunate man" if he could avoid the danger. Thereafter he was called *MacRatha*, "the fortunate son."
>
> It is true that this clan was an ancient stock in Ireland and had great estates there in olden days, and have produced eminent men and are still numerous in that island.
>
> The name here is spelled MacRa, but varies by the region where any of the clan generally reside. There are various ways of spelling this name: thus in Ireland, they use MacRath and Macgrath; in the north of Scotland, MacRah, MacRae, MacCraw and MacCrow. In England and the south of Scotland, the Mac is left out from an ill-founded prejudice, and the name Rae, Craw, Crow, and such like, are of the same stock.[9]

The Origin of the Mackintoshes

The following extract from the history of the Mackintoshes was originally written in Latin by Lachlann Mackintosh of Kinrara in about the year 1680. Like some of the other chroniclers, he says that he is eager to intervene in the representation of clan history so that he can set the record straight, and he bolsters his own authority by demonstrating his knowledge of previous historians of high regard.

> What has chiefly moved me to expend my labor on these genealogies, and on the collecting of observations – nay, the very thing itself, if I may so speak, to be kept in view in the whole of this matter – is that I

may make clear to all Mackintoshes and Chattans, ignorant of their origin, the true knowledge of their descent. ...

BENEVOLENT READER,

If you should doubt the truth of the statements which are made in this epitome (especially concerning the origin and antiquity of the Mackintoshes), you should know that such arguments, documents, and testimonies as are accustomed, for the most part, to be adduced for the origin of kingdoms, republics, cities, and ancient peoples whatsoever (namely, chronicles, annals, histories, writings of old scribes, and traditions universally received), these are alleged in evidence of the origin of this family.

Mackintosh, as George Buchanan says in book 17 of his *Rerum Scoticarum*, was the chief of a great family among the ancient Scots. These are the very words of Buchanan, and they show, not only the original surname but also that the family was sprung from the ancient Scots. ...

Ailpin, King of Scots, was taken in battle, not far from Dundee by Brude, King of the Picts, and shortly after cruelly beheaded, and his head fixed on a pole set up in the most conspicuous place of Abernethy, the chief town of the Picts, to mock him. Kenneth, second son of Ailpin, so swiftly took out vengeance against the Picts for the slaughter of his father that, their forces having been vanquished in many fierce battles, he at length expelled them all from Britain and added the Kingdom of the Picts to his empire in the year 839.

The Picts, having been thus destroyed, he divided the lands formerly occupied by them among his own people ... he gave a district then called Otholinia to Fife Duff, a man noble and warlike, and sprung from the ancient Scots ... Henceforth, this country was named Fife, as a lasting memorial of the deeds strenuously done by Fife Duff.

This Fife Duff was the first Thane of Fife, and progenitor of all the Thanes and Earls of Fife of the surname MacDuff. ...

Shaw, second son of Duncan, the third Earl of Fife, was appointed by King Malcolm IV of Scotland as the constable of the castle of Inverness. While he dwelt there he was commonly called by the neighbors Shaw *Mac an Tòisich* "the son of the Thane," and in this manner the surname Mackintosh had its start from him, and passed on to his posterity.[10]

The Origin of the Buchanans

William Buchanan of Auchmar wrote a history of the Buchanans, from which this extract comes, no later than the year 1723. This account underscores the shared Gaelic society spanning the Irish Sea – Ulster and Argyllshire being separated by a very short span of water – and the symbolic importance of the Norse as a unifying enemy.

This text illustrates how the personal names of successive chieftains (or other leaders) sometimes spawned a number of different surnames. This is also one of the first references to the *sluagh-ghairm*, a name or phrase that was used to rally the members of the clan to a specific place in the case of an emergency or battle muster. This also contains an early description of the *crois-tàraidh* or *crann-tàra* "summoning stick," usually referred to in English as the "fiery-cross" (although it was a charred stick and was not aflame when in use).

> Absolan Buidhe Ó Cathain, son of Ó Cathain, the provincial king of the southern part of Ulster, left Ireland about the year 1016 and landed with some attendants on the northern coast of Argyllshire, near the Lennox. He was introduced to King Malcolm II of Scotland by a nobleman who had a considerable interest in those parts and had the king's favor. The King took him into his service against the Norse and he distinguished himself particularly in two battles against them.
>
> In recompense for his services, Ó Cathain obtained several lands in the north of Scotland. ...
>
> This Absolan Ó Cathain is reputed to be the progenitor of that surname, first laird of Buchanan. His son and successor was called Eòin, who was given a charter of the Wester Mains of Buchanan, granted by Ailín, first earl of the Lennox, in the reign of King Malcolm III. ...
>
> MacBeatha was the sixth laird of Buchanan. This personal name was ordinary among the MacAbsolans, before the assumption of the surname Buchanan, as also among those of the sept of that surname, who have retained their ancient denomination. ...
>
> It was Absolan the third of that name and seventh laird of Buchanan who first assumed the surname of Buchanan. ... He obtained from Maol Domhnaich, Earl of the Lennox, a charter of an island in Loch Lomond called Clàr Innis. ...
>
> The isle of Clàr Innis was the *sluagh ghairm* ("war-cry") proper to the family of Buchanan; such like being usual in all other families in these

times and for some following ages. So soon as this call was raised upon any alarm, the word Clàr Innis was sounded aloud from one to another, in a very little time, throughout the whole country; upon hearing of which all effective men belonging to the laird of Buchanan with the utmost diligence repaired well armed to the ordinary place of rendezvous which, when the lairds resided in that island, was upon a ground on the opposite shore.

That which in these more modern times came in place of the *sluagh ghairm* was the fire-cross, being a little stick with a cross on one end of it, the extremities of which were burnt, or made black by fire. This cross, being once set a-going, was carried through with such speed as in a few hours would alarm the people of a vast extent of territory.[11]

The Origin of the Grants

The following extract is from a history of the Grants written by Seumas Chapman, Minister of Cromdall, in about the year 1729. This account draws from a text sent from the court of Denmark to the Grants, which explains its heavy and unusual emphasis on Norse ancestry. Perhaps the Danes who compiled this imaginative version of Grant origins were using these genealogical claims to reforge links with Scotland after the 1707 union with England, given that the new political arrangement weakened Scotland's ties to Scandinavia and the rest of the continent of Europe.

> Wffa was a Saxon lord descended from the champion Odin and the first king of the East Angles. Hacken, Earl of Lagen, was descended from Wffa, and was renowned for his power and conduct not only in Sweden and Denmark but also in Norway, where he was unanimously chosen as Lord High Protector of that kingdom … He was called "Hacken Grandt" alias Grant or Grott, which in their language is the same as "great" or in Latin "Grand" is Great or Valorous, and all his Posterity after him are commonly called Grants. …
>
> Hacken Grant the Protector of Norway married Suanhilla the daughter of Swenerman, a Danish prince, of whom he begat several children.
>
> Hemming Grant, his second son, is the progenitor of the house of Grant. He married Tora, daughter to Adlistein, the first of the Norwegian kings who professed the Christian religion. Among others instructed in the same religion were Hemming and his wife Tora, which was disagreeable to his father Hacken the Protector, seeing that they did abandon the heathenish custom of worshipping and offering sacrifice to his progenitor Odin, reputed among them formerly as a god.

Hemming being thus made uneasy by his father thinks fit to remove with his wife Tora out of Norway and come to Ireland, where his said lady died in exile, leaving behind her several sons and daughters. ...

Hemming Grant is said to have four sons who came along with him and afterward thought fit (upon their father marrying a second wife named Isobella, daughter to the Prince of Dublin) to push their fortunes and came to Scotland in the year 1000.

The four sons are said to be Allan, Gregor (who is said to be the progenitor of the MacGregors), Fingon (the progenitor of the MacKinnons) and Rowan alias Ruthven "red-haired," who is the progenitor of the Ruthvens.[12]

The Origin of the MacLeans

The following extract comes from a history of the MacLeans written by Dr. Eachann ("Hector") MacLean of Gruline, Mull, in 1734. The account reflects the reality that the MacLeans were vassals of the Clan Donald Lords of the Isles and that the dissolution of the Lordship unleashed the latent rivalries between numerous clans across the Western Highlands and Islands.

> The surname *MacGilleEathain* "Son of GilleEathain" is derived from one GilleEathain, predecessor of the family. He was called *GilleEathain na Tuaighe* "GilleEathain of the Axe" from his ordinary weapon, a battle axe, which his posterity to this day bear in their crest between a laurel and cypress branch.
>
> Regarding this GilleEathain we have nothing on record, nor is there any tradition concerning him that can be much relied on, and by this space of time we cannot fix on the place of his residence or what character he had in the world, only that by the universal consent of tradition that a Gael of that name was predecessor of those families called after him MacGilleEathain. This family had their *seanchaidh*s and bards, as every family of distinction in the Highlands had. ...
>
> GilleEathain begat GilleÌosa who begat GilleChaluim, whose son was called Eòin Dubh, whose sons were called Lachlann Lùbanach, predecessor of the family of Duart, and Eachann Reaganach, predecessor of the family of Loch Buidhe. ...
>
> About the beginning of the reign of Robert the Third, King of Scotland, which was in the year 1390, those two brothers, Lachlann Lùbanach and Eachann Reaganach, came, as some say, from Ireland to

MacDougall of Lorne's house. They were kindly received and obtained much of MacDougall's favor, and after some time suffered the fate of all foreign favorites, which is generally to be hated by those who think themselves injured by such intruders. They went so far as to bring MacDougall at last into a plot to take away the lives of the brothers.

They gave their enemies the slip and came to the great MacDonald of the Isles. Here again their good behavior procured them MacDonald's favor. But, as in the former case, they again began to be hated by those who were afraid of their obtaining too much favor.

The first who vented his ill-will to them was the Laird of MacKinnon, speaking harshly to them when he returned from hunting where they had been with MacDonald. They resolved revenge when an opportunity should offer itself, which in a little time did in this manner.

MacDonald went from Àros in Mull to the mainland on some expedition, sailing away. The Laird of MacKinnon was to follow, but the brothers killed him as he was going onboard, manned his galley, and followed MacDonald, resolving to make their fortunes or die in the attempt.

As soon as they came alongside of him, they boarded and made him prisoner, carrying him to the island of Garbh Eileach. After giving them his promise, they brought him to Iona. Here he vowed friendship to them upon certain stones, called the Black Stones, where men used to make solemn vows, and granted them lands by charter which they and their successors enjoyed afterward.[13]

How the MacDonalds Got Possession of Dalness

The following tale was originally collected in Gaelic from Archibald Campbell of Benderloch in the mid-nineteenth century. The incidental details in the story illustrate that hunting was a right jealously guarded by the clan that was granted official ownership of an estate and that land ownership could be transferred from one family to another by the use of charters.

> *Dail an Eas* ("The Field of the Waterfall," called "Dalness" in English) is situated at the head of Glenetive, and includes the magnificent twin mountains called the *Buachaillean* ("Herds") which, rising from the same base, and having between them only the narrow pass of *Làraig Ghartain*, stand like giant sentinels at the head of the glen. It lies contiguous to *Am*

Monadh Dubh ("Black Mount") and has from time immemorial been famed as a deer-forest.

The property of *Dail an Eas* belonged at one time to the Livingstons of Achanacree in Benderloch, a family that appears to have held a good position in their day. On a certain day Livingston's three sons went to Dail an Eas to hunt deer. On the same day one of the MacDonalds of Glencoe went there for a similar purpose, except that he was a trespasser. By careful stalking he succeeded in killing a deer.

In their wanderings through the forest the Livingstons came upon him and saw what he had done. Leaving the deer behind him, he immediately took to flight, making for the hill with all the speed of which he was capable. The Livingstons set off in pursuit, perhaps motivated by the recollection of former depredations, if not by clan animosity.

When they found that he was likely to outstrip them, one of them bent his bow and shot an arrow, which entered MacDonald's heel. Plucking it out, MacDonald, though suffering keenly from the wound, fled with unabated speed until he came to the slope that leads down to Achatriochadain.

The sons of the laird of Achatriochadain, having observed the plight their MacDonald clansman was in, hid themselves until the Livingstons were past them. They then closed in on them, cut off their retreat to Dail an Eas, and took them prisoners.

The first impulse of the MacDonalds was to kill the Livingstons, but the wounded hunter would not permit it.

"Let us," he said he, "take measures with them that will be of greater advantage than killing them. Let two of them be detained as prisoners and the other sent to Achanacree for the charters of Dail an Eas."

This was done. In the course of a few days the charters arrived, and the property of Dail an Eas passed forever out of the hands of the Livingstons. The three young men were then allowed to return home.[14]

The Origin of the MacIver Campbells

The following tale was originally collected in Gaelic in the mid-nineteenth century and illustrates how a chieftain's title and surname were derived from the founder of a branch of a clan, as well as how lands could be subdivided between sons.

The Earl of Argyll had a brother called *Ìomhar Crosg* ("Cross-grained Iver"), between whom and the Earl some dispute arose. Ìomhair left in anger, going to Lochawe-side, among the MacCallums, where he and the MacCallums plotted the death of the Earl, whereby Ìomhair was to become chief and the MacCallums were to get more lands. A feast was to be held, to which the Earl was to be invited.

The Earl accepted the invitation, but he took care to be well armed, having his helmet and coat of mail, and claymore (or two-handed sword). At the feast all vied with each other in simulated loyalty and devotion to Argyll. After the feast was over, they gave the Earl the best bedroom they had, which was just a barn; and two sentries were placed at the door, in order, as they pretended, to secure the Earl's comfort, but really in order to make certain that the Earl should not escape alive.

Tired after the feast, the Earl lay down to rest, having his coat of mail on and his sword by his side. He was awakened by feeling the coat of mail burning his skin, for the barn was on fire. He rose up, and with one kick made the wicker door of the barn fly open with such force as to alarm the sentinels, who fled. The Earl plunged into a river close at hand, and, walking to the stable, took to his horse and rode away.

Ìomhair, some time after this, returned to Inverary, when the brothers again became friends. The lands of Ardkinglas were granted to Ìomhair, extending from Lochfynehead to Lochgoilhead, and down the south shore of Loch Long to Kilmun.

From this Ìomhair are descended the MacIver Campbells of Lochgair and Asknish. His son and heir was called *Iain Riabhach* (Brindled John), and since then the chief of Ardkinglas was known in Gaelic as *Mac Iain Riabhaich*, son of Brindled John.[15]

The Origin of the Macintyres of Glennoe

Most tales about the founding of clans and the acquisition of estates focus on top-down power structures and use of force and violence. The following tradition, about the relocation of a branch of the Macintyres (whose origin legend is given above) to inland Argyllshire, was collected in the late nineteenth century. It is an unusual example of an origin legend in which a community (rather than a single "heroic" leader) relies upon the aid of a supernatural ally for success. The white cow in this tale is an ancient Celtic archetype ultimately related to the sacred cattle of Hindu tradition.[16]

The Macintyres came from one of the Western Isles. They lived for some time south of Ben Cruachan. They tried on several occasions to drive their cattle through the passes of that mountain but were always stopped and turned back by a spirit that acted as guardian of the mountain.

This spirit, however, was by no means unfriendly to them. It told them one day that they had been taking the wrong passes and directed them to the pass or opening that led to Glennoe. It also told them to follow a white cow that they had in their herd and to build a house for themselves on the first spot on which the cow would lie down to rest.

They followed its advice. The result was that they settled in the beautiful valley of Glennoe.[17]

---

[1] Campbell, "The Manuscript History," 187.

[2] MacGregor, "Writing the History," 357-59.

[3] Adapted from Cameron, *Reliquiæ Celticæ*, vol. 2, 155-57.

[4] Adapted from MacPhail, *Highland Papers*, vol. 2, 5-7.

[5] MacGregor, "Writing the History," 366.

[6] Adapted from MacPhail, *Highland Papers*, vol. 1, 6-7.

[7] MacGregor, "Writing the History," 368.

[8] Adapted from MacPhail, *Highland Papers*, vol. 2, 72, 73, 74-75, 76-77, 79.

[9] Adapted from ibid, vol. 1, 198.

[10] Adapted from Clark, *Genealogical Collections*, vol. 1, 145, 146, 153-54, 156.

[11] Adapted from Buchanan, *Account of the Family of Buchanan*, 158-59, 162, 164, 165-66.

[12] Adapted from Clark, *Genealogical Collections*, vol. 1, 103-05.

[13] Adapted from ibid, 118, 121-22.

[14] Adapted from Campbell, *Records of Argyll*, 117-19.

[15] Adapted from ibid, 67-68.

[16] Newton, *Warriors of the Word*, 235.

[17] Sinclair, "The Macintyres of Glennoe," 291.

Chapter Five

Everyone Has Their Place
Social Structures, Roles, and Landholding

This chapter will enable you to answer the questions:
- How was the clan system organized?
- Were clans really large, extended families or were they made of other sorts of social units and relationships?
- What social classes and professional roles existed in clan society?
- What was the relationship between people and the land that they occupied?

Kinship: Biological and Contractual

Clans are usually assumed to be large, extended families commanded by patriarchs. This popular notion is not entirely wrong-headed given that the clan system emerged from Gaelic society, which was very kin-oriented, and the word *clann* itself means "children." The idea that a clan is an actual family is a vast oversimplification, however, of the relationships between those who were in these social units, how they were actually organized, and how they changed over time.

It was usually only the leaders of the clan – the chieftain and lateral branches of the clan founder – who were biologically related. The other people in the clan were often not related in genealogical terms but could have been brought into the social unit by marriage, fosterage, friendship, or contractual arrangements.

It would be more accurate to think of clans like corporations run by presidents who were selected from a pool of qualified descendants of the founder. These "corporate leaders" competed with one another to attract people into their employ by offering attractive rewards for their services. Once accepted into the group, clan members would be more likely to invest their efforts for the communal good, marry within its ranks, and strive for its success.

Clans were social organizations in which all members worked together in all aspects of their lives for the greater good of their community, sharing human, natural, territorial, and cultural resources.

> Indeed, politics, economy, marriage, kinship, possession of land and of property, were all woven together into an inextricable web in Highland society, to produce a culture which was both dynamic and self-perpetuating. Principal and subordinate clans were interlocked through marriage, not only at the higher levels, but also at the local level, minor *clann* becoming established by marriage in territory dominated by another clan ...[1]

Over time and through communal experience, the sense of belonging to a clan, for people at all levels of the social hierarchy, could grow quite strong, especially because it was such a close-knit group with many interdependencies. In fact, the constant intercourse between social classes and Gaelic customs of succession created a society which had a remarkably high percentage of nobles in comparison with most of the rest of Europe.[2] The fluid intercourse between all members of a clan is illustrated by many tales, songs, and proverbs in Gaelic tradition.

It was exactly these deep bonds of allegiance and trust that made clansfolk feel utterly betrayed and violated when their former-chieftains-turned-landlords began evicting and transporting them in the eighteenth century. The strong bonds between families in a community gave them a strong preference to emigrate together in large groups, and attempt to reconstitute their communities in exile, into the early twentieth century.

Although kinship was the organizing principle of Highland clan society, not everyone in the same clan was biologically related in reality: a variety of social and legal arrangements was used to draw new kin-groups into a clan or allow them to break off and form new bonds with other families. Modern-day scholars refer to this way of thinking as *fictive kinship*. An anonymous, late seventeenth-century commentator tells us that Gaels of that era were conscious of these principles: "They reckon him to be their chief, whom they choose for their patron: tho he be not of their name."[3] This demonstrates that the "clan system" was not focused solely or even primarily on blood kinship but on many forms of bonds which, by the early sixteenth century, became increasingly based on formal, written contracts. Families sometimes even created fake genealogies to insert themselves into the clan to which they allied themselves in order to maintain the fiction of kinship.[4]

Marriage is a nearly universal means of uniting kin-groups and was particularly important as a political arrangement at the upper echelons of Gaelic society; the lower orders enjoyed much more freedom of choice in marriage partners because the political implications were less important. A bride's family contributed a *tochradh* "dowry" (borrowed into Lowland Scots as "tocher") when she married. A wife was entitled to recover the value of her dowry in the case of divorce. Marriage was one of the ways in which clans sought to gain wealth and territory, and such wealth could be lost when a daughter left her kin-group.[5]

Fosterage was the most important form of non-biological kinship in the Highland clan system. With deep roots in Gaelic society that go back to the Celtic Iron Age, fosterage created bonds between families, bonds that were considered even more sacrosanct than blood. There are numerous anecdotes and tales in Gaelic tradition about parents who injured their biological children to death – or showed willingness to do so – because they did not meet their obligations to their foster-siblings. Such cautionary tales underline the social imperative of fosterage in Gaelic society, as is also reflected in the Gaelic proverb "*Co-dhaltas gu ceud, is cairdeas gu fichead*" ("Fostership to the hundredth degree, kinship to the twentieth degree").[6] It was similarly noted in a seventeenth-century document that "They reckon a Foster Brother Dearer to a man than his own Brother & will dye for one an other."[7]

The bond of *manrent* was another form of fictive kinship which became increasingly common by the late fifteenth century. Manrent was a form of clientage in which a man (sometimes as a representative of his kin-group) entered into a formal contract with a superior chieftain or regional lord; the dependent offered his loyalty and services (and that of his clan) to a more powerful lord in exchange for the latter's protection and leadership. The prevalence of manrent contracts illustrates that kinship by itself was insufficient to maintain the social order of clanship.

The *comh-cheangal* "bond of friendship" was generally contracted between peers for mutual assistance, usually because of common military and political interests. They could also be contracted at the resolution of a feud to prevent future conflict between families.[8]

Clan society is commonly portrayed as a kind of classless democracy; in fact, until its collapse in the late eighteenth century, Gaeldom was stratified and highly conscious of inherited status. Society was ordered and operated according to social rank, especially when exhibited in public form. Judging by the evidence of oral tradition, the aristocrat was the object of attention – and, generally, affection – among his peers and dependents. People took pride in their connections, of all sorts, with the élite; many popular songs composed by females of the lower classes boast of the love-children of high-born men, for example. The literary tradition itself is imbued with values and practices formed by and for the élite.

Anglophone culture has stereotyped Highlanders as wild, lawless barbarians, a perception that is largely the result of the disenfranchisement of Gaeldom from power in Scotland as well as the history of ethnic antagonism. The Lordship of Isles (under the rule of Clan Donald in the fourteenth and fifteenth centuries) was able to maintain law and order under a centralized Gaelic authority, but the destruction of the Lordship released bloody rivalries that the Scottish Crown was eager to exploit. Some clans (especially the Campbells and MacKenzies) acted as agents for the central government and often manipulated disorder and provoked hostile reactions from competing clans for their own benefit. In short, as the contrasts between the anglophone world and the Gaelic world increased, so did the negative typecasting of Gaels as primitive savages who needed to be conquered and reformed for their own good.[9]

Roles and Professions

The descendants of Somerled were beginning to establish or endow religious orders in Scotland as early as the thirteenth century. In later generations, both his male and female descendants became leading clergy in the church, which gave them access to considerable power: by the fifteenth century, the church in Gaelic Scotland had become closely entwined with politics. The patronage of the Lords of the Isles was also crucial in maintaining the expenses of bardic training and practice, as well as that of other learned classes, who tended to pass on these specialties within their own family. Among the professionals in the employ of the Lord of the Isles were MacMhuirich ("Currie") poets, MacMhuirich ("Morrison") lawyers, MacDhubhShìdh ("MacDuffie") archivists, MacBheatha ("Beaton") medical doctors, and MacGilleSheanaich ("Shaw") harpers.

It was common for people to move between different high status professions. Members of the MacMhuirich poetic dynasty, for example, also became doctors and clergymen. The Lordship's support enabled Gaelic culture to flourish in a stable and nurturing environment, resulting in an era recalled later as *Linn an Àigh* "The Golden Age." The account of the Campbells of Craignish remarked on the trained professionals managing the roles of historian and public-relations manager for clans in these terms:

> It's well known to any that have but the least smatterings of (knowledge of) the old Scottish affairs that every considerable family in the Highlands had their *bard*s and *seanchaidh*s. The *bard* was the family poet and the *seanchaidh* their prose writer, but very often the *bard* supplied the place of both. These offices were heritable and had a pension, commonly a piece of land annexed to that office. Their work was to hand down to posterity the valorous actions, conquests, battles, skirmishes, marriages and relations of the predecessors by repeating and singing the same at births, baptisms, marriages, feasts and funerals, so that no people since the curse of the Almighty dissipated the Jews took such care to keep their tribes, cadets, and branches so well and so distinctly separate.[10]

Large-scale and long-term warfare created a demand for a professional class of warrior mercenaries. From the late thirteenth century onwards, Irish leaders, especially in their resistance to English conquest, recruited heavily from the *gall-óglaigh* warriors of the Highlands and Islands (usually called "galloglasses" in English) and in exchange, the chieftains of large clans imported learned professionals trained in the churches and bardic colleges of Ireland.

The chieftain kept ranks of trained fighting men called *buannachan* and a bodyguard of chosen warriors called *léine-chneas* (or *léine-chnios*). New recruits from the *tuath* "peasantry" were sometimes taken into this privileged profession on account of their renowned strength or prowess.[11] Military hosts were raised at short notice in the Highlands by a series of messengers passing along the fiery cross (as described in the text about the origin of the Buchanans given above).

Land-Holding

A powerful chieftain created a network of kinsmen and allies to hold down his territory; this pattern of land-holding basically imposed the social structure of a clan upon the landscape. Privileged members of the clan could be offered the office of "tacksman" (variously called *fear-baile, fear-fearainn* or *fear-taca* in Gaelic). These middle managers of one or more townships were given such duties as collecting rents, organizing military operations, and supervising the exploitation of agricultural resources. As lawyer William Fraser commented in 1772, the role of tacksman provided a place and function for the many clan élite, for a chieftain

> gave Leases of their Land to their younger Sons and other Connexions, and very seldom to any but their own name and Kindred – The Tacksmen formed a kind of inferior Gentry in the Country and their rents were often little more than an acknowledgement to their Chief or head of their family.[12]

A clan's wealth ultimately depended upon the amount of productive territory under its control, but productivity was measured in terms of social value rather than the monetary value of surplus goods exported for sale. Land was necessary for growing crops and grazing livestock which fed the men who defended these lands and sought to expand their holdings. Clans could acquire new land peaceably by marriage or royal favor, or forcibly by conquest.

The kin-groups loyal to a chieftain, whether through real or fictive kinship, did not always occupy a cohesive, well-bounded territory: they were often spread out over a patchwork of dispersed estates. Some kin-groups were able to expand their territory, while others were forced by circumstances or more successful neighbors to shrink or relocate. Some kin-groups occupied land owned by a chieftain other than their own and paid rent to him, on top of the tribute given to their chieftain. Chieftains could also find themselves with a bonanza of new land because of grants given by the king or regional magnates. Chieftains needed to be able to respond dynamically to fluctuations in their territorial command and those of their subordinates.

When a chieftain suddenly needed to control a new expanse of territory, his first choice was generally to fill it with kinsmen loyal to him as subordinates – brothers, sons, other clan élite. These kinsmen in turn brought their dependents and tenants to occupy and work the land. This could result in mass displacement of the previous population. Pre-existing tenants sometimes resisted these evictions forcibly, even resorting to sustained guerrilla warfare that lasted for years.

A chieftain did not always have sufficient clients or kin to distribute upon his estates, however. In such a case he used the social mechanisms of fictive kinship – manrent and friendship in particular – to forge new bonds to provide him with new subordinates he could enlist into clan affairs. Some of these could have been tacksmen and their tenants already occupying the land who were willing to accept a new chieftain as their landlord. The territory of a clan was seldom composed exclusively of members of one kin-group, but contained a complex patchwork of tenants of differing ancestry and territorial origins.

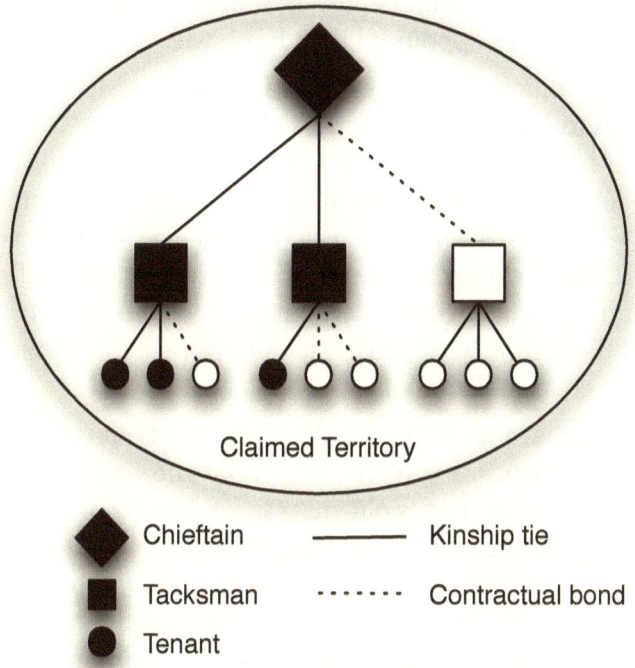

Figure 5.1: Social structure and territorial occupation

Figure 5.1 above depicts a hypothetical example of a chieftain's use of social networks and fictive kinship to occupy and control territory. Members of the clan who are related are darkened. The chieftain brings in two tacksmen related to him by kinship; some of their tenants were already in the territory and were unrelated to them. The chieftain also forms a contractual bond of manrent with a tacksman already in the territory (the rightmost square) whose tenants give their loyalty and service to the new chieftain.

Primary Sources

Fosterage Contract of Tormod MacLeòid

This contract was originally written in Gaelic in 1614 on behalf of Sir Ruairidh Mór MacLeòid, chieftain of the MacLeods of Dunvegan

1590-1626, so that his son Tormod (anglicized as "Norman") could be fostered by a man named Eòin MacKenzie. One of the four witnesses to this contract, Toirdealbhach Ó Muirgheasa, was a member of a poetic dynasty attached to the MacLeods. Besides Tormod, the contract also mentions Sir Ruairidh's appointed heir, Eòin, who in fact succeeded him.

> This is the condition and agreement under which MacLeod is giving his son Tormod to Eòin son of MacKenzie, and this is the condition under which Eòin has him: if it happens that Eòin dies first, his wife will keep the child until she gets a husband for herself, but the guardianship of the child will go to Aonghus son of MacKenzie so long as he remains unmarried, and as soon as a man marries her, Angus will get the child from that time forward for the duration of his life. If his brother, Domhnall the son of MacKenzie, lives longer than Aonghus, Domhnall shall get the child in like manner.
>
> MacLeod will have a child's worth of the assets during the lifetime of the three – himself, his son the heir (Eòin the son of MacLeod), and Tormod this foster-son of Eòin the son of MacKenzie – against Eòin, and against Aonghus son of MacKenzie, and Domhnall son of MacKenzie, and against the two sons of Domhnall the son of Murchadh, namely, Ruairidh and Murchadh, and against the two sons of Donnchadh the son of Domhnall, namely, Eòin and Domhnall, and against Brian son of MacMhuirich, and against GilleChaluim MacPherson.
>
> This is the property which Eòin son of MacKenzie put in the possession of the child Tormod: four mares, and another four which MacLeod put in his possession, along with three mares which he promised to him when he took him in his care. Eòin son of MacKenzie shall be the caretaker of these seven mares which MacLeod gave to the child, so that they may flourish for his foster-son. MacLeod shall likewise be caretaker of the four mares which Eòin son of MacKenzie gave to his foster-son so that they may flourish for him in like manner.
>
> These are the witnesses to this: Mr. Eóghan MacSuibhne, minister of Diùirinis; Domhnall son of Black Paul; Eòin MacColgain, minister of Bracadale; Toirdealbhach Ó Muirgheasa; on the eighth day of October, in the year of our Lord one thousand six hundred and fourteen.[13]

Martin Martin, *A Description of the Western Isles*

Martin Martin (*c*.1660-1719) was a native of the Isle of Skye who was educated at the University of Edinburgh and wrote a tract about the

Hebrides in about 1695 that was intended to give the central authorities a more favorable and optimistic view of Gaelic islanders than they generally held and a sense of the human and natural resources that could be developed in the region, if political policies and relationships could be improved. Being a native Gael himself, his many detailed comments provide a rare insider's view of matters in this era.

The first excerpt from his volume provides fascinating insight about the cattle raid as a rite of passage and test of leadership for an aspiring chieftain. A later passage describes the ritual for forming a bond of friendship.

> Every Heir, or young Chieftain of a Tribe, was oblig'd in Honour to give a publick Specimen of his Valour, before he was declar'd Governor and Leader of his People, who obey'd and follow'd him upon all Occasions.
>
> This Chieftain was usually attended by a Retinue of young Men of Quality, who had not beforehand given any Proof of their Valour, and were ambitious of such an Opportunity to signalize themselves.
>
> It was usual for the Captain to lead them, to make a desperate Incursion upon some Neighbour or other that they were in Feud with; and they were oblig'd to bring by open force the Cattel they found in the Lands they attack'd, or to die in the Attempt.
>
> After the Performance of this Atchievement, the young Chieftain was ever after reputed valiant and worthy of Government, and such as were of his Retinue acquir'd the like Reputation. This Custom being reciprocally us'd among them, was not reputed Robbery, for the Damage which one Tribe sustain'd by this Essay of the Chieftain of another, was repair'd when their Chieftain came in his turn to make his Specimin: but I have not heard an Instance of this Practice for these sixty Years past. ...
>
> Their antient Leagues of Friendship were ratify'd by drinking a Drop of each other's Blood, which was commonly drawn out of the little Finger. This was religiously observ'd as a sacred Bond; and if any Person after such an Alliance happen'd to violate the same, he was from that time reputed unworthy of all honest Mens Conversation.
>
> At the first Plantation of these Isles, all matters were manag'd by the sole Authority of the Heads of Tribes, call'd in the Irish *Tighearna*, which was the same with *Tyrannus*, and now it signifies Lord or Chief; there being no Standard of Equity or Justice, but what flow'd from

them. And when their Numbers increas'd, they erected Courts call'd *Mòd*, and in the English, Baron-Courts.

The Proprietor has the Nomination of the Members of this Court; he himself is President of it, and in his absence his Bayliff: the Minister of the Parish is always a Member of it. ...

The Heads of Tribes had their Offensive and Defensive Leagues, call'd *Mandrate*, and *Manrent* in the Lowlands; by which each Party was oblig'd to assist one another upon all extraordinary Emergencies. And tho the Differences between those Chieftains involv'd several Confederates in a Civil War, yet they oblig'd themselves by the Bond mention'd above to continue stedfast in their Duty to their Sovereign.[14]

Bonds between MacRaes and Campbells

The following legal document, called a "contract of friendship" in the original text, was drawn up between the MacRaes of Kintail and the Campbells of Craignish in the year 1702. It specifies their mutual obligations and clarifies cases of conflicts of loyalty at the highest level of government.

> ... the firm, stable and sure love and favor the said Farquhar MacRa and others foresaid, of the said name of MacRa, and their predecessors did and doth bear to the said George Campbell of Craignish and his predecessors, and the acts of kindness and friendship done by the said name of MacRa to the said family of Craignish, when occasion offered, in all time bygone.

> And now for the more firm and sure upholding and maintaining of the said relationship, friendship and correspondence, and for the better keeping and preserving the same on record, in all time coming, the said George Campbell of Craignish, by their presents, binds and obliges him, his heirs and successors, to maintain and in hand take the part of any of the said name of MacRa, in all lawful causes, and defend the same to the utmost of their power, against any other person, their duty to Her Majesty and her Highness' successors and Council, and their immediate lawful superiors always excepted.

> And such like the said Farquhar MacRa, Mr. Donald, Donald, John, Duncan and Kenneth MacRa, in name and behalf forsaid, for them their heirs, and all others lineally descending of their bodies, by their presents, binds and obliges them and their foresaids, so far as they may do by law, to own, maintain, and in hand take the part of the said

George Campbell of Craignish or his foresaids, or any others lineally descending of his Family, in all lawful causes, and defend any of the said Family, to the utmost of their power, against all other person or persons, their duty to Her Majesty and Her Highness' successors and councell and their immediate lawful superiors, all is excepted.[15]

Edmund Burt, *Letters from the North*

This extract of Burt's letter from the 1720s demonstrates the hierarchical nature of Highland society and the intense loyalty expected of clansfolk for their chieftain, which is why the central government considered Highland clans to constitute a threat against their own authority.

> The Highlanders are divided into tribes, and clans, under chiefs, or chieftains, as they are called in the laws of Scotland; and each clan again divided into branches from the main stock, who have chieftains over them. These are subdivided into smaller branches of fifty or sixty men, who deduce their original from their particular chieftains, and rely upon them as their more immediate protectors and defenders. But for better distinction I shall use the word "chief" for the head of the whole clan, and the principal of a tribe derived from him I shall call a "chieftain."

> The ordinary Highlanders esteem it the most sublime degree of virtue to love their chief, and pay him a blind obedience, although it be in opposition to the Government, the laws of the kingdom, or even to the law of God. He is their idol; and as they profess to know no king but him (I was going further), so will they say they ought to do whatever he commands without inquiry.

> Next to the love of the chief is that of the particular branch from which they sprang; and, in a third degree, to those of the whole clan and name, whom they will assist, right or wrong, against those of any other tribe with which they are at variance, to whom their enmity, like that of exasperated brothers, is most outrageous.[16]

Rev. John Macpherson, *Critical Dissertations*

The first part of this excerpt concerns the practice of native Gaelic law – or at least its later derivative form – in the Scottish Highlands. This law system was, from the first records in the early medieval period, one focused more on payment for the damage committed to victims than punishment of the perpetrator. Macpherson is rather dismissive of civil law in the Highlands, but we should keep in mind that with the abolishment of the

Lords of the Isles in 1495 and the English conquest of Ireland in the early seventeenth century, the native Gaelic law schools were undermined and customary law would have been a much less formal and regulated set of practices, lacking a central authority committed to Gaelic norms to oversee and reinforce the exercise of laws.

The rest of this excerpt testifies to the vital role that poets and poetry played in Scottish Highland political life, and the services that they were expected to provide for their chieftains.

> The *Brehon* or *Breitheamh* may be ranked, without any impropriety, among the old Scottish titles of honour. The Brehons were, in North Britain and Ireland, the judges appointed by authority to determine, on stated times, all the controversies which happened within their respective districts. Their courts were usually held on the side of a hill, where they were seated on green banks of earth. These hills were called "mote hills."
>
> It may be presumed that the Brehons were far from being deeply skilled in the intricate science of the law, which they professed. By conversing with the ecclesiastics in their neighbourhood, they learned some scraps of the canon law, but knew little or nothing of the civil. The customs which prevailed in the land wherein they lived, and the opinion of the times, were generally their rules of decision. The office belonged to certain families, and was transmitted, like every other inheritance, from father to son. Their stated salaries were farms of considerable value.
>
> By the Brehon law even the most atrocious offenders were not punished with death, imprisonment, or exile, but were obliged to pay a fine, called *éirig*. The eleventh or twelfth part of this fine fell to the Judge's share: the remainder belonged partly to the king, or superior of the land, and partly to the person injured; or if killed, to his relations. ...
>
> It is needless to prove that the Gaels had the greatest value for poetry. Never did any nation encourage or indulge the profession of bards with a more friendly partiality. Their nobility and gentry, their kings, both provincial and supreme, patronized, caressed, and revered them. The bards of a distinguished character had estates in land settled on themselves and their posterity. Even amidst all the ravages and excesses of war, these lands were not to be touched, the poets own person was sacred, and his house was esteemed a sanctuary.
>
> Every principal bard was in the Gaelic tongue called *file* or *ollamh*, that is to say, a doctor in poetry. Each of the great *file*s or graduates had thirty

bards of inferior note constantly about his person, and every bard of the second class was attended by a retinue of fifteen poetical disciples. ...

About a century back one of the Highland chieftains retained two principal bards, each of whom had several disciples who were his inseparable attendants. The chieftains of former times, if led by choice, or forced by necessity, to appear at court, or join those of their own rank, on any public occasion, were attended by a numerous retinue of vassals, and by their most eminent poets and ablest musicians. ...

The chief bards of North Britain, like those of other Celtic nations, followed their patrons into the field, and were frequently of signal service. It was their business and custom, upon the eve of a battle, to harangue the army in a war song composed in the field. This species of a song was called *Brosnachadh Catha*, that is to say, an inspiration to war.[17]

Rev. Donald MacQueen, "A Dissertation..."

Reverend Donald MacQueen was the minister of Kilmuir, the Isle of Skye, when he wrote the essay "A Dissertation on the Government of the People of the Western Isles" in 1774. The latter part of this excerpt describes the inter-dependencies between people and the ways in which the emphases on honor and shame – especially as amplified by the poets, who praised good behavior and satirized bad – helped to reinforce moral behavior.

> They had a Sheriff of the Isles under the Norwegian dynasty; but when the lands were parcelled out afterwards by the Lords of the Isles, the descendants of Somerled, among barons of different ranks and sizes, each of these barons, assisted by the chief man of the community, held his court on the top of a hill called *Cnoc na h-Éirig* "the Hill of Pleas," where the disputes they had among themselves were determined, where the encroachments of their neighbours were considered, and the manner of repelling force by force, or the necessary alliances they were to enter into, resolved on. ...
>
> All the time preceding the beginning of the fifteenth century, and somewhat later, the government of the Isles and of the neighbouring continent was of the military kind. The people were made up of different clans, each of which was under the direction of a chief or leader of their own, and as their security and honour consisted in the number and strength of the clan, no political engine was neglected, that could be thought of, to increase their numbers or inflame their courage.

The children of the principle people were given out to nurses: the foster-brothers, or *comh-dhaltan*, as they called them, with their children and connections for many generations, were firmly attached to their will and interest. This sort of relation was esteemed a stronger bond of friendship than blood or alliance. ...

A quick sense of honour and shame, which was nourished by their education, being all bred to the use of arms, to hunting, to the exertion of their strength in several amusements, games and feats of activity. The bard celebrated the praises of him who distinguished himself on any of these occasions, and dealt out his satire, but with a very sparing hand, for fear of rousing up the ferocity of men, who were in use to judge in their own cause, when they appealed to the sword, and either retrieved their honour, or died; valour was the virtue most in repute; according to their progress in it were they distinguished by their chieftain and friends.

Every one of the superior clans thought himself a gentleman, as deriving his pedigree from an honourable stock, and proposed to do nothing unworthy of his descent or connections; and the inferior clans, the *bodaich*, as they called them, tread at an humble distance in the steps of their patrons, whose esteem and applause they courted with passionate keenness. The love, affection, and esteem of the community all aimed to procure by a disinterested practice of the social duties, truth, generosity, friendship, hospitality, gratitude, decency of manners, for which there are no rewards decreed in any country, but were amply paid among the Highlanders by that honour and respect of which they had a very delicate taste.[18]

Rev. John Buchanan, *Travels in the Western Hebrides*

The Reverend John Lane Buchanan was a native Gael born in Menteith, on the southern edge of the Highlands. He traversed the Western Isles as a missionary for the Society for the Propagation of Christian Knowledge from 1782 to 1790. In this passage he comments on the practice of fosterage and how it created and sustained bonds between families, sometimes for considerable periods of time.

The lower order of people value themselves much on their connections with the rich. Connections often arise from the time that a mother, wife, or sister, gave suck to the gentleman's child; whence they call them *comh-dhaltan* or fosterlings. This appellation is used by all the family, as well as by the child whose mother's milk suckled the great man's child. This familiar epithet is no less useful to the rich than to the poor man because, if the rich man countenances the poor, the last, in return, will think himself interested in protecting the flocks, and other effects of the rich; so that this tie of friendship being reciprocally useful, is continued for generations.[19]

Anne Grant, *Essays on the Superstitions* and *Letters*

In these excerpts from her essays and letters, Anne Grant describes her understanding of the most fundamental social bonds in Highland life and how those attachments provided constraints and incentives for moral behavior.

> She (a wife) borrowed a kind of sacredness from the tie which united her to her husband ... independent of mental charms or personal attractions, was endeared to the husband by this tacit homage, and by a tie, more prevalent by far here, than in polished societies. She was the mother of his children; to her he was indebted for the link that connected him with the future descendants of his almost idolized ancestors.

> No Highlander ever once thought of himself as an individual. Amongst these people, even the meanest mind was in a manner enlarged by association, by anticipation, and by retrospect. In the most minute, as well as the most serious concerns, he felt himself one of the many connected together by ties the most lasting and endearing. He considered himself merely with reference to those who had gone before, and those who were to come after him; to these immortals who lived in deathless song and heroic narrative; and to these distinguished beings who were to be born heirs of their fame, and to whom their honours, and perhaps, their virtues, were to be transmitted. ...

> In every narrow vale, where a blue stream bent its course, some hunter of superior prowess, or some herdsman whom wisdom had led to wealth, and wealth to power, was the founder of a little community, who ever after look'd up to the head of the family as their leader and their chief. Those chains of mountains which form'd the boundaries of their separate district had then their ascents cover'd with forests, which were the scene of their hunting excursions. When their eagerness in pursuit of their game led them to penetrate into the districts claim'd by the chief of the neighbouring valley, a rash encounter was the probable consequence, which laid the foundation of future hostilities.

These petty wars gave room to a display of valour and conduct in the chiefs, and produc'd a still closer cohesion and mutual dependence among their followers. These hasty animosities were soon hush'd into peace, yet often renew'd. The consequence was that the clans became expert in arms, cautious, vigilant, and enterprising. They form'd alliances, offensive and defensive, cemented them by intermarriages between the chief families of the confederating clans, governed their followers by a kind of polity not ill-regulated, and the chief had the power of life and death over all his large family (for such he considered his clan), but this was very sparingly us'd.

In cases of long feud and much mutual exasperation, a chieftain might be cruel to his enemies, but never to his friends. To their own people they were invariably clement and indulgent. Nor were these paternal rulers in any sense so despotic as they have been represented; so far otherwise, that of all monarchs they were the most limited, not being permitted to take a step of the least importance without consulting their friends. By this expression was meant the elders of their tribe, including relations so distant, that in any other country they would not be recognis'd as such. But then in this council of elders, those who were not regarded as prudent and sagacious persons had no weight.

It can scarcely be imagined by us, who depend not so much on the wisdom of our sages, how nicely they weighed and discriminated the degrees of intellect, and how carefully the wise or witty sayings of these oracles were treasur'd up and delivered down to posterity. The poor laird could neither marry or give in marriage, raise a benevolence or levy war without the full consent of these counsellors, who, unless he happen'd to be a man of uncommon talents, govern'd him much more than he did them. He led out the tribe no doubt, but then they led out the families of which the tribe consisted, and unless perfectly satisfied with the ground of quarrel they would not move.

The celerity with which they sometimes appeared in the field, was rather a proof of the unanimity of the clan than the despotism of the chief. ...

... their peculiarly social mode of living together, the address necessary to conciliate and adjust jarring interests among allied clans, and the habit of making all private considerations subservient to the good of the community, sharpened their native sagacity and enlarged their minds. Meantime their excessive delight in poetry, music, and the tales in which the heroic deeds of their ancestors were preserv'd, communicated to their imaginations a tender and romantic enthusiasm, which gave a high and peculiar colouring to their affections and their virtues. ... it is undeniably certain that remains, undoubtedly genuine, of poems compos'd by the bards attach'd to certain great families, within these three or four centuries, still exist sufficient to do honour both to the genius and the virtues of this secluded people.

These remains are peculiarly valuable for the high strain of heroic generosity and pure morality which breathe thro' them ... It is to be observ'd to the honour of those untaught bards that their wild strains of eulogy and lamentation never fail'd to wait upon departed merit, however deprest or unfortunate. No highland worthy ever died 'uncelebrated or unsung.'[20]

---

[1] Ommer, "Primitive Accumulation," 126.

[2] Patterson, *Cattle Lords & Clansmen*, 11-12; Munro, "The Clan System," 121; Grant, *Highland Folk Ways*, 11-12.

[3] Campbell, *A Collection of Highland Rites*, 57; Hunter, *The Occult Laboratory*, 65.

[4] Dodgson, *Age of the Clans*, 16.

[5] Patterson, *Cattle Lords & Clansmen*, 310-1; Stiùbhart, "Women and Gender," 235-7.

[6] Nicolson, *Gaelic Proverbs*, 29.

[7] Campbell, *A Collection of Highland Rites*, 57; Hunter, *The Occult Laboratory*, 65.

[8] Dodgshon, *From Chiefs to Landlords*, 34, 40.

[9] Newton, *Warriors of the Word*, 24, 26-32, 130, 149-50.

[10] Adapted from Campbell, "The Manuscript History," 190.

[11] Newton, *Warriors of the Word*, 126, 155.

[12] Quoted in Dodgshon, *From Chiefs to Landlords*, 95.

[13] My translation of the original Gaelic text in Cameron, *Celtic Law*, 224-25.

[14] Martin, *A Description of the Western Isles*, 101-02, 109, 124-25.

[15] Adapted from MacPhail, *Highland Papers*, vol. 1, 207-08.

[16] Simmons, *Burt's Letters*, 191-92.

[17] Macpherson, *Critical Dissertations*, 169-70, 193-94, 199, 201-02 (emending "Irish" to "Gaelic").

[18] Pennant, *A Tour In Scotland*, 746, 751-2.

[19] Buchanan, *Travels in the Western Hebrides*, 114.

[20] Grant, *Essays on the Superstitions*, 50-52; "Mrs. Grant's Letters," 299-300, 302-03.

Chapter Six

The Bare Necessities
Food, Clothing, and Shelter

This chapter will enable you to answer the questions:
- How did Scottish Highlanders make effective use of the resources in their environment to feed, clothe, and house themselves?
- How did Scottish Highlanders perceive their own way of life, environment, and material conditions?

Living in a Material World

Human beings need a minimum of food, clothing, and shelter to survive. The ways in which these fundamental requirements are satisfied are limited by the resources available in the environment, but each society makes its own selective and creative use of the possible options and constructs its own solutions according to its own values, judgments, and cultural-specific reasoning.

It is a fact of geography that the landscapes of Highlands and Western Isles of Scotland present great challenges to people attempting to make a living in them: little of the land is suitable for agriculture, the winters can be long and fierce, many areas are exposed to harsh winds, the depletion of the forests made timber scarce, and so on.[1]

Nonetheless, the obsession of anglophone writers with materialism and their unwillingness to allow Gaels to speak for themselves has distorted the representation of the Highlands and the way of life of Scottish Gaels with stereotypes of barbarity and poverty. It would be more constructive and rewarding to focus on understanding how Highlanders managed to create a rich and meaningful culture, and sustainable way of life, with the limited resources available to them. After all, they loved the land in which they lived dearly, identified with it, and defended it with their lives, as the stories and songs that they tell themselves testify to us.

The cattle economy was one of the key Gaelic solutions to this ecological challenge: while most of the soil is poorly suited to the cultivation of crops, it is well suited to the grazing of cattle and other livestock. A range of dairy products produced from their milk was the main food source, but the cattle were sometimes bled, with the blood being mixed with oatmeal to make black pudding, and some were slaughtered for their meat.[2] Manure served as fertilizer on arable fields worked in the village[3] (as was the thatch removed from houses in the Outer Hebrides[4]). Cattle also served as an export product to trade for goods needed from elsewhere.[5]

Figure 6.1: Drawing of a thatched house in the Highlands, drawn in 1790

While there were many common practices and elements of material culture across the Highlands, there are also many regional variations as communities adapted to the resources, climate, and conditions specific to their own environment. They supplemented their diet, for example, with the foods available in their local environment, as depicted in the recollections of a Highlander who grew up near the Dornach Firth (given below in the Primary Sources section).

Fashions changed over time, often facilitated by the introduction of new materials into the Highlands. One example of this was cochineal, a dye imported from the Americas in the seventeenth century in order to turn wool a bright red. This color was particularly popular among the Highland élite who could afford it (as in the lament for Iain mac GilleChaluim in the Primary Sources section below).

The tartan plaid is strongly associated with Highlanders in the popular imagination, but even clothing techniques and styles have evolved over time in Gaelic Scotland. The word "tartan" is probably derived from the Old French word *tiretaine*, used to describe a cloth made of wool and linen. The Gaelic word *breacan* "speckled thing" has been in use since at least the eighth century to describe checkered textiles worn as clothing or used as blankets and bedding. Combining yarn into checkered patterns was a natural solution for distributing yarn so that color irregularities were not immediately obvious. This technique, in fact, is found all around the world from the earliest times and has the added benefit of allowing weavers to design their own patterns.[6]

The traditional kilt, called *féileadh mór* in Gaelic and often "the belted plaid" in English, seems to have evolved in about the sixteenth century. A lengthy strip of woolen cloth is pleated in the middle and held together at the waist with a belt; the excess material is then folded around the body to keep the wearer warm in the extreme weather to which the Highlands are often subject. The song-poem *"Am Breacan Ullach"* ("The Proud Plaid") given below offers a highly detailed description of the belted plaid.

Figure 6.2: Drawing of a thatched house in the Highlands, drawn in 1866

The belted plaid – long and bulky – could become a hinderance in battle, however. Highlanders often let it drop from them in war, fighting in "just the shirts on their backs," as in this description of the MacLeans of Mull in 1674: "MacLean of Bròlas and his accomplices, to the number of seven score armed men, armed with firelocks, swords and targets, in a posture ready to fight, with their plaids thrown from them."[7] It should also be kept in mind, however, that trousers – called *triubhas* in Gaelic and "trewes" in Scots – have been a fashion item amongst the Gaelic élite for even longer than the kilt.

Figure 6.3: Drawing of Highland clothing in the eighteenth century

The environmental challenges faced by Highlanders, and the solutions they created to solve them, were similar to those of other peoples of northern regions, but Gaelic cultural norms and traditions make the folkways of the Highlands unique in many ways.

Primary Sources

Finlay the Red-haired Bard, *"My Favorite Big-House"*

Fionnlagh am Bard Ruadh ("Finlay the Red-haired Bard") was a professionally trained poet who was in the employee of Eòin ("John") MacGregor, the chieftain of Clan Gregor, in the later fifteenth century. As is clear from the poem, he also paid an official visit to the court of Aodh MacDiarmada on the Rock of Loch Cé in Connacht, Ireland, whose house he compares to the great hall of the MacGregors.

This translation of a Classical Gaelic praise poem, taken from the Book of the Dean of Lismore, is a very rare depiction of the dwelling of a Highland chieftain in the medieval period. Unfortunately, the manuscript is damaged and a few words are missing. The middle of the poem applauds the generosity of the Irish chieftain MacDiarmada for allowing an uninvited guest to partake of his hospitality for a year, maintaining that MacGregor is no less generous. The poem concludes with gratitude for MacGregor's wife Elizabeth for her support.

> I found my favorite big-house
> In which the poet-bands feast:
> Great companies choose that residence
> That is never found forlorn on any day.

> I will boast, since they are in his house,
> The fortress of the dragon of the Scottish capital:
> Every massive, smooth door in the house,
> On which the light of day and night are equal.

> (Missing) feasts,
> And from its expansive architecture,
> The poet-bands do not find it cramped,
> Although containing all of the household makes it so.

> The heroic feats of his hounds and his war-bands
> Are frequently made by Eòin of the blood-red weapons;
> Leaving home in pursuit of the hunt,
> He leaves every meadow red from the kill.

> The carpenters accomplished fine work
> On MacGregor's wood-framed residence;
> We find no flaw of masonry
> Since you have entered the space.

> Wine is being imbibed by ladies at leisure,
> O MacGregor, in your great hall;
> It seems to me, in your strong, spacious abode,
> That candle wax is ablaze as far as the door post.

> I found a residence to compare to your own,
> O MacGregor of the capital of Scotland:
> The royal residence of the long blades,
> The home of Aodh MacDiarmada.

> There was a day when the gentle-souled man,
> MacDiarmada of the Rock,
> Encountered an unpleasant creature in his residence,
> Having evaded the retinue of his stronghold.

97

After coming into his house
MacDiarmada set the hag
To the wattled side of the house,
That cloaked apparition of a hag.

Strewn out in the bright residence,
A bed was made for the mischief-maker,
Unsought by the household;
She spent a year lying there by herself.

No one asked her
What land she hailed from
All that year in his residence,
Belonging to MacDiarmada.

She arose at the end of the year –
A tale for which there is evidence –
And that misshapen hag
Became a young, shapely maiden.

Neither is anyone rejected from your home,
O MacGregor, no guest at all,
From your elegant dwelling – all know it –
Any more than that grey-haired hag of the Rock.

(Missing) I will send
To Aodh's home a sign of honor;
That is no insult to Ireland,
That the palace of the poet-bands is here in Scotland.

Both sides of your home are expansive,
With many residents;
Hundreds of royal revelers on its floor,
Great the harp music and ancient song-lays.

I will not be absent:
I receive fine gifts in your great house;
Of the residences of Gaels on this side of the ocean,
This is my favorite of all I have found.

Elizabeth of the kind soul,
The daughter of John son of Archibald,
Does not exclude poet-bands from her home;
She is a lady full of hospitality and generosity.

The foster-mother of the poet-bands and chiefs

Is Elizabeth of Glenlyon;
A refined lady, most hospitable of women;
I believe she found an excellent spouse.[8]

George Buchanan, *The History of Scotland*

This extract from scholar George Buchanan's 1582 treatise on Scottish history, translated from Latin to English, offers an early description of the food, clothing, and housing of Scottish Highlanders, particularly those of the non-élite classes.

> In their food, clothing, and in the whole of their domestic economy, they adhere to ancient parsimony. Hunting and fishing supply them with food. They boil the fish with water poured from the paunch or skin of the animal they kill and in hunting sometimes they eat the flesh raw, merely squeezing out the blood. They drink the juice of the boiled flesh. At their feasts they sometimes use whey, after it has been kept for several years, and even drink it greedily; that species of liquor they call bland, but the greater part quench their thirst with water.
>
> They make a kind of bread, not unpleasant to the taste, of oats and barley, the only grain cultivated in these regions, and, from long practice, they have attained considerable skill in moulding the cakes. Of this they eat a little in the morning, and then contentedly go out hunting, or engage in some other occupation, frequently remaining without any other food till the evening.
>
> They delight in variegated garments, especially striped, and their favourite colours are *purpureum* (dark red, purple) and *caeruleum* (blue, green-blue). Their ancestors wore plaids of many different colours, and numbers still retain this custom, but the majority, now, in their dress, prefer a dark brown, imitating nearly the leaves of the heather, that when lying upon the heath in the day, they may not be discovered by the appearance of their clothes; in these, wrapped rather than covered, they brave the severest storms in the open air, and sometimes lay themselves down to sleep even in the midst of snow.
>
> In their houses, also, they lie upon the ground; strewing fern, or heath, on the floor, with the roots downward and the leaves turned up. In this manner they form a bed so pleasant, that it may vie in softness with the finest down, while in salubrity it far exceeds it; for health, naturally possessing the power of absorption, drinks up the superfluous moisture, and restores strength to the fatigued nerves, so that those who lie down

languid and weary in the evening arise in the morning vigorous and sprightly.[9]

Unnamed MacLeod, "Lament for Iain mac GilleChaluim"

Iain Garbh mac GilleChaluim MacLeod of the island of Raasay was drowned on 19 April 1671. According to tradition, one of his sisters composed a lament for him every Friday for a year after his death. The following is a translation of one of those songs which she composed. It offers an intimate portrait of her brother, his physical features, clothing, and skills, and the impact of his death on others. He is described as wearing a bright-red tartan suit with trews (trousers). His mastery of the bow and arrow are also striking details.

> Look out, and see if it is daytime,
> As I attend the skyline;
>
> It is bitter news
> That was told to me after Easter.
>
> Your retinue was drowned on the rocks
> Along with your brother Calum.
>
> You were a great man of Torcall's lineage,
> Strong was your body.
>
> Tartan suits you well
> Shining with red cochineal dye;
>
> No less do trews suit you
> To go strolling the streets.
>
> Tonight intense grief for you
> Lies heavy on the Earl of Kintail.
>
> That the sea-winds were against you
> As you rode it out at its worst.
>
> Climbing out on the point
> You were scourged in a way that I dislike.
>
> You were sullied by sea foam,
> Coming from the ocean, drowned.
>
> It has preoccupied my mind
> So that I am made sleepless into the morning.
>
> I would enjoy so much of your affection
> When I would come to your hall.

Very handsome was it above your kilt:
A sharp, shiny Spanish sword.

With a lubricated scabbard,
And a smooth shield on your left side.

A ready hand for the archery target
That would not go awry as much as a churl's pinafore.

With the fresh, broad belly of the bow,
That would knock down the wooden marks.

Even if all (Highlanders) were present
You would receive the highest honor.[10]

Anonymous, *A Collection of Highland Rites and Customs*

It is not clear who wrote this important account of the common customs and rituals of Scottish Highlanders that was copied by the Welsh antiquarian Edward Lhuyd, but it appears to have been originally compiled in about 1685.[11] Although these notes are short and often cryptic, they provide valuable nuggets of information about Scottish Gaelic folklore and social customs in the seventeenth century.

> Their ordinary habit at home is their Trewes and when they goe abroad they use belted playd; and short hose. The woman's playd is belted also and sides to the ground. They wear a Broach on the Breast of Silver or Brasse according to their Quality. The poorer women wear nothing but their plaid. Their plaids serve them for Bed-covering, Bodily cloathing; Towel, Sayls, Mortclaith, etc. …
>
> They use to put on the right foot hose and the Right foot shoe first. …
>
> Their houses for the most Shields made of earth or stone & clay & riveted with Rivets. In Loch Aber the Walls of their houses is of Juniper & such like pletted together. …
>
> In the time of scarcity they launce their cows neck and make meat of their blood.
>
> The Lochabermen when they Kil a Cow, hang up the whole carcase, and eat it as they need.
>
> When they are in the Hills they boyl their Flesh in the skin with a fire of the bones or other Fuel. They boyl also the Flesh in a Haggis.
>
> The live most on milk & Fishes.

They (in the Isles especially) have a way of drying their corn before it be threshen, by burning the straw & it together, keeping the corn very dextrously from being wrong'd with the Fire; then they grind it in Querns.

The Gentleman's Bread is made like a Triangle: The commons of a round Form. ...

Except that they may eat a litle in the morning, usually they eat none til night, when they come in from their labour.[12]

Martin Martin, *A Description of the Western Isles*

Martin Martin, writing in about 1695, gives us extensive and interesting details about Highland clothing and domestic architecture, including the evolution of the kilt in the late sixteenth century. He also notes that class distinctions were becoming widely felt during the seventeenth century in the Highlands, with the upper classes imitating the styles of the Lowlands. His observation that the patterns of tartans reflected regional styles and habits lends further proof, if any were needed, that there was no system of clan tartans.

> There are only five Families in this small Island (Rona), and every Tenant hath his Dwelling-house, a Barn, a House where their best Effects are preserv'd, a House for their Cattle, and a Porch on each side of the Door to keep off the Rain or Snow. Their Houses are built with Stone, and thatched with Straw, which is kept down with Ropes of the same, pois'd with Stones. ...
>
> (In St. Kilda) The distance between their Houses is by them called the High-street: their Houses are low built, of Stone, and a Cement of dry Earth; they have Couples and Ribs of Wood covered with thin earthen Turff, thatch'd over these with Straw, and the Roof secur'd on each side with double ropes of Straw or Heath, pois'd at the end with many Stones: their Beds are commonly made in the Wall of their Houses, and they lie on Straw, but never on Feathers or Down, tho they have them in greater plenty than all the Western Isles besides. The Reason for making their Bedroom in the Walls of their Houses, is to make room for their Cows, which they take in during the Winter and Spring. ...
>
> The first Habit wore by Persons of Distinction in the Islands, was the *Léine-Cróich*, from the Irish word *Léine*, which signifies a Shirt, and *Cróich* Saffron, because their Shirt was dyed with that Herb: the ordinary number of Ells us'd to make this Robe was twenty four; it was the upper

Garb, reaching below the Knees, and was tied with a Belt round the middle: but the Islanders have laid it aside about a hundred Years ago.

They now generally use Coat, Wastcoat, and Breeches, as elsewhere; and on their Heads wear Bonnets made of thick cloth, some blue, some black, and some grey.

Many of the people wear Trowis: some have them very fine woven like Stockings of those made of Cloth; some are colour'd, and others striped: the latter are as well shap'd as the former, lying close to the Body from the middle downwards, and tied round with a Belt above the Haunches. There is a square Piece of Cloth which hangs down before. The Measure for shaping the Trowis is a Stick of Wood, whose Length is a Cubit, and that divided into the Length of a Finger, and a half a Finger; so that it requires more skill to make it, than the ordinary Habit.

The Shoes antiently wore, were a piece of the Hide of a Deer, Cow, or Horse, with the Hair on, being tied behind and before with a Point of Leather. The generality now wear Shoes, having one thin Sole only, and shaped after the right and left Foot; so that what is for one Foot, will not serve the other.

But Persons of Distinction wear the Garb in fashion in the South of Scotland.

The Plad wore only by the Men, is made of fine Wool, the Thred as fine as can be made of that kind; it consists of divers Colours, and there is a great deal of Ingenuity requir'd in sorting the Colours, so as to be agreeable to the nicest Fancy. For this reason the Women are at great pains, first to give an exact Pattern of the Plad upon a piece of Wood, having the number of every Thred of the Stripe on it. The Length of it is commonly seven double Ells; the one end hangs by the Middle over the left Arm, the other going round the Body, hangs by the end over the left Arm also: the right Hand above it is to be at liberty to do any thing upon occasion. Every Isle differs from each other in their Fancy of making Plads, as to the Stripes in Breadth, and Colours. This Humour is as different thro the main Land of the Highlands, in so far that they who have seen those Places, are able, at the first View of a Man's Plad, to guess the Place of his Residence.

When they travel on foot, the Plad is tied on the Breast with a Bodkin of Bone or Wood, just as the Spina wore by the Germans, according to the Description of C. Tacitus: the Plad is tied round the middle with a Leather Belt. It is pleated from the Belt to the Knee very nicely: this dress for Footmen is found much easier and lighter than Breeches, or Trowis.

The antient Dress wore by the Women, and which is yet wore by some of the Vulgar, called *Earrasaid*, is a white Plad, having a few small Stripes of black, blue, and red; it reach'd from the Neck to the Heels, and was tied before on the Breast with a Buckle of Silver, or Brass, according to the Quality of the Person. I have seen some of the former of a hundred Marks value; it was broad as any ordinary Pewter Plate, the whole curiously engraven with various Animals, &c. There was a lesser Buckle, which was wore in the middle of the larger, and above two Ounces weight; it had in the Center a large piece of Chrystal, or some finer Stone, and this was set all round with several finer Stones of a lesser size.

The Plad being pleated all round, was tied with a Belt below the Breast; the Belt was of Leather, and several Pieces of Silver intermix'd with the Leather like a Chain. The lower end of the Belt has a Piece of Plate about eight Inches long, and three in breadth, curiously engraven; the end of which was adorned with fine Stones, or Pieces of Red Coral. They wore Sleeves of Scarlet Cloth, clos'd at the end as Men's Vests, with Gold Lace round 'em, having Plate Buttons set with fine Stones. The Head-dress was fine Kerchief of Linen strait about the Head, hanging down the Back taper-wise; a large Lock of Hair hangs down their Cheeks above their Breast, the lower end tied with a Knot of Ribbands.[13]

Edmund Burt, *Letters from the North*

These extracts from the letters of Edmund Burt provide some interesting details about houses and domestic architecture in the Highlands, even if he has a rather dismal view of them. In the first excerpt, a company of Englishmen are confused and angered by a Highlander who tells them that they will see the "castle" of a chieftain from a high vantage point, which turns out to be a humble building made of turf. Burt also notes that only the homes of chieftains closer to the Lowlands or near the ocean tended to be built of stone.

> However, at last we gained the Height; but when we were there, one of our Company began to curse the Highlander for deceiving us, being prepossessed with the Notion of a Castle, and seeing only a House hardly fit for one of our Farmers of fifty Pounds a year; and in the Court Yard a Parcel of low Outhouses, all built with Turf, like other

Highland Huts. When we approached this Castle, our Chief with several Attendants (for he had seen us on the Hill), came a little Way to meet us; gave us a Welcome, and conducted us into a Parlour pretty well furnished. ...

The latter part of what I have written of this letter relates chiefly to gentlemen who inhabit the Hills not far from the borders of the Lowlands, or not very far from the sea, or communication with it by lakes; as, indeed, most part of the houses of the chiefs of clans are in one or other of these situations. These are sometimes built with stone and lime, and though not large, except some few, are pretty commodious, at least with comparison to these that are built in the manner of the huts, of which, if any one has a room above, it is, by way of eminence, called "a lofted house;" but in the inner part of the mountains there are no stone buildings that I know of, except the (British military) barracks; and one may go a hundred miles an end without seeing any other dwellings than the common huts of turf. ...[14]

Alasdair mac Mhaighstir Alasdair, "The Proud Plaid"

Alasdair mac Mhaighstir Alasdair ("Alexander MacDonald" in English) was a key figure in the 1745 Jacobite Rising and one of the most important and innovative Gaelic poets of the eighteenth century. He composed a Gaelic song-poem, usually called *"Am Breacan Uallach"* ("The Proud Plaid"), not long after the Battle of Culloden, defiantly reveling in the tartan and belted plaid.

The central government passed the Act of Proscription (also known as the "Disarming Act") in 1746 in an effort to demilitarize the Scottish Highlands. It made it illegal for civilian men to wear tartan and kilts, thus divesting them of their native fashions and a traditional means of expressing masculinity. This poem personifies the plaid, describing many aspects of rural life in the Highlands of the time. It is also important to note that propagandists such as Alasdair mac Mhaighstir Alasdair promoted the tartan as a symbol of the Jacobite cause itself.

> I would much prefer the proud plaid,
> Around my shoulders, and under my arm,
> Rather than any coat I could get
> Made of the finest fabric that comes from England.
>
> The uniform is my own treasure,
> That which must be closed with the belt;
> Quilting up the plaid

After arising to go on a journey.

The tidy plaid of the folds,
Favored is the heroic clothing;
I would travel the fresh-water springs with you
Throughout cold mountains, and handsome are you on the field.

The proper attire of the soldier
Sensible at the time of marching;
You are handsome in the battle advance,
Under the whirring of the bagpipes and the banners.

You are no worse when charging into battle
When the sword scrapes out of the scabbard;
The true garb of the rout
In order to energize the feet!

You are good for hunting the deer
When the sun rises on the rocky summit,
And I would depart sprightly with you
Going to the village on Sunday.

I would lie down with you snugly
And I would leap up as brisk as a deer with you;
I would be quicker to my weapons
Than a Redcoat with a clunky musket.

When it's time for the cock to crow
On a knoll in the dewy morning,
You'd come in much better use
Than a lousy, ragged coat.

I would travel with you to a wedding,
Never touching the dew of the grass;
Lovely is the garment
In which the young bride took great pleasure.

You are exhilarating in the forest,
Covering me with your warmth and protection
From snow and mist,
You would defend me against rain showers.

Gracefully on top of it
Would the studded shield lay,
And the claymore on a handle belt
Slanted above your pleats.

A musket complements you nicely,
Fitting merrily under my arm;
And despite rain and calamity
And torrent, you shelter me.

You are good in the night,
Excellent as bed-clothes;
I would prefer you over the finest, most costly
Sheets of linen that are in Glasgow.

Neat, elegant, beautiful
At weddings and gatherings is the tartan;
Lifted up is the flowing cloth
With a shoulder pin to hold it.

You were good by day or by night,
You were striking on mountain and shore;
You were good at war and at peace –
No true king would proscribe you.

He thought that this (act) would wear down
The blade of the agile Gaels
But instead he has sharpened them
Keener than the edge of the razor.

He left them full of malice,
As ravenous as starving hounds;
No drink can satisfy their thirst,
Not even wine, only the true blood of England.

Even if you were to rip the heart out of us
And tear apart our chests,
We will not be parted from Prince Charles,
Ever, until our last breath.

He is entwined into our souls,
Knit as tightly as locks;
He cannot be unfastened from us
Until he is reaped out of us.

Just like a woman in child-birth
Who labors until delivery,
Rather than rejecting him
She intensifies her passion for her spouse.

Even if you (the government) have shackled us

With tight bonds, to prevent our movement,
We will run as swiftly
And as constantly as deer in vegetation.

We keep to our ancient constitution
As we were before the Act;
In body and mind
And in loyalty to king, we will not grow weak.

The blood that ran through our ancestors' veins
And the courage of their hearts
Was left to us as an inheritance:
Be loyal! That is our religion.

Curses on everyone
Who is still not willing to rise with you;
Regardless of whether he is clothed
Or bare naked to his skin.

The manly youth is my darling
Who has gone across the water from us;
The warmest wishes of your country
And their prayers follow you.

Although you (Redcoats) got the upper hand
This one time by accident,
The Devil is always at war:
The Butcher (Cumberland) will get another fight.[15]

Rev. John Buchanan, *Travels in the Western Hebrides*

As a fellow Gael, the Reverend John Lane Buchanan felt great sympathy for the suffering of the people of the Outer Hebrides and the deteriorating conditions he found there. He expresses his outrage frequently in the book he published in the hopes that his reading audience would find a way to alleviate the causes of the hardships of the Gaels, especially the unchecked and rising power of landlords and their agents.

> The *sgallag* builds his own hut with sods and boughs of trees; and if he is sent from one part of the country to another, he moves off his sticks, and, by means of these, forms a new hut in another place. He is, however, in most places, encouraged by the possession of the walls of a hut, which he covers in the best way he can with his old sticks, stubble, and fern. ...

A nourishing root is commonly dug up by the poor, in time of scarcity, out of the arable lands, called *brisgean* or wild sherrat, and when boiled, answers the purpose of bread or potatoes: they are also prohibited from this as much as possible. Digging or opening the lands for these roots exposes the field to be blown away by the drift. Here are carmile roots, wild carrots, baldmony, hemlock, heath, rushes, strawberries, blackberries, cranberries, juniper-berries, and several other wild fruits. ...

The men wear the short coat, the *féileadh beag* "short kilt" and the short hose, with bonnets sewed with black ribbons around their rims, and a slit behind with the same ribbon in a knot, Their coats are commonly tartan, striped with black, red, or some other colour, after a pattern made, upon a stick, of the yarn, by themselves, or some other ingenious contriver. Their waistcoats are either of the same, or some such stuff; but the *féileadh beag*s are commonly of *breacan*, or fine Stirling plaids, if their money can afford them.

At common work they use either short or long coats and breeches made of striped cloth, and many of them very coarse, according to their work. Their shirts are commonly made of wool and however coarse they may appear to strangers, they are allowed to conduce much to the health and longevity for which this country is famous; as I have known them eighty, ninety, and some even a hundred years old, in these islands, and able to do their daily work. ...

Their brogues (shoes) are made of cow or horse leather, and often of seals skins, that are commonly well tanned by the root of tormintile, which they dig out from the hillocks, and uncultivated lands, about the sea-side. This, properly pounded and prepared, without either lime or bark, is sufficient to make the hides pliant and fit for wearing. It answers their purpose much better than leather tanned with lime or bark, because they seldom grow hard or shrink when dried, even though wet all day; which is not the case with such as are burnt with lime. They never use tan-pits, but bind the hides fast with ropes, and hold them for several days in some remote solitary stream, until the hair begins to come off, of its own accord; and after that, the tormintile roots are applied for bark, as above described. ...

The women wear long or short gowns, with a waistcoat and two petticoats, mostly of the stripes or tartan, as already described, except the lower coat, which is white. The married wives wear linen mutches, or caps, either fastened with ribbons of various colours, or with tape straps, if they cannot afford ribbons. All of them wear a small plaid, a yard broad, called *guileachan*, about their shoulders, fastened by a large broach.

The broaches are generally round, and of silver, if the wearer be in tolerable circumstances: if poor, the broaches, being either circular or triangular, are of baser metal and modern date. The first kind has been worn time immemorial even by the ladies.

The *earrsaid*s are quite laid aside in all this country, by the different ranks of women; being the most ancient dress used by that class. It consisted of one large piece of flannel, that reached down to the shoe, and fastened with clasps below, and the large silver broach at the breast, while the whole arm was entirely naked.

The ladies made use of the finer, while common women used coarser kinds of flannel, or white woollen cloths. The married women bind up their hair with a large pin into a knot on the crown of their heads, below their linens; and the unmarried frequently go bare-headed, with their hair bound up with ribbons, or garters. ...

Frequently the old women wear little *guileachan*s (small plaids) about their shoulders, and woollen hoods about their heads, with very coarse linen under them fastened with a pin below their chins. The *bréid*, or curtah, a fine linen handkerchief fastened about married women's heads, with a flap hanging behind their backs, above the *guileachan*, is mostly laid aside. ...

Every subtenant must have his own beams and other side timbers. Four or five couples, with their complement of side timbers, are reckoned a good sufficiency for a hut. The walls of them are six feet thick, packed with moss or earth in the middle, with a facing of rough stones built on both sides. This is called a stall, and commonly belongs to the master: upon this the timbers are erected, as follow:

First, the beams and spars are bound together by ropes made of heather or bent, and placed standing on these stalls. Then the side rafters are fastened with ropes to those beams pretty fast, and the rows of ropes wrought very close, so as to keep the stubble with which the houses are thatched from falling through. For the beams and roof-tree, with the side timbers, could not bear the weight of divats above them, and therefore the ropes must be the thicker plaited over them.

Having laid the stubble over the side timbers, interwoven with ropes, they secure this thatch with heather ropes thrown across the roof of the huts, and these are fastened below with large stones which are fixed to their ends, and hang dangling over the sides of the wails to keep all fast, that the winds and storms, which are frequent here, may not strip the huts of their covers.

They burn the straw of the sheaf, to make the oats dry for meal: and though the grain is black by the ashes, and the meal coloured, yet it is not unpleasant to the taste, and it is thought to be very wholesome food. This, with most of their oatmeal, they grind on *bràth*s a kind of mill similar to the quern, but made of harder stone, and of the same magnitude with quern millstones, being about three feet in diameter, and four or five inches thick. The uppermost stone is turned round by the hand of one or two women, who grind as much meal, evening and morning, as serves for the day.

They have also some of the old Highland mills, that are driven about by water. Those mills are rude, and extremely simple in their constructions, being only one wheel that drives round the spindle, which is fastened to the upper grinding millstone. These mills are slow, and at such distances from the huts of the tenants, that in general they prefer their *bràth*s or querns.

Their cakes are made of barley meal, and toasted against a stone placed upright before a good fire; and sometimes, when either haste or hunger impels them, they are laid on the ashes, with more ashes above, to bake them more quickly. The people eat twice a day. The first meal is called *dinnear* or breakfast, the last is their supper. They seldom break fast, unless from some necessary haste, before eleven o'clock; and the supper, when night drives them home from their labour, is placed before them.

The tenants repair to the hills all Summer with their cattle, and live in shealings; that is, in huts, made in the hills for the Summer residence of those who tend the flocks and herds. There the families live mostly on milk, butter, and cheese, and fish; and by the time they return to their farms, the grass about their corn fields becomes excellent, and makes the cows yield plenty of milk.[16]

Sarah Murray, A Companion and Useful Guide

Sarah Murray of Kensington was an English gentlewoman who travelled the north of Britain in the late 1700s and wrote a travelogue intended to guide other travelers. Although she was often appalled by the material conditions she found, she also praises Highlanders for their virtuous behavior. In this excerpt, she describes the temporary habitations that women and children built while they attended the cattle at the summer grazings.

The eight miles from High Bridge to Fort William, is the most dreary, though not the ugliest, space I had travelled in Scotland. It is very thinly inhabited; and notwithstanding its non-productive appearance, I never drunk finer milk than I did there, from cows I found milking on the road's side; and what was still more extraordinary, though I gave it but a trifle more value of what was drunk, the honest creatures though it *too much*, though they *seemed* the poorest of the poor in Scotland.

The huts on this moor are very small and low, are soon erected, and must very soon fall down. They consist of four stakes of birch, forked at the top, driven into the ground; on these they lay four other birch poles, and then form a gavel at each end by putting up more birch sticks, and crossing them sufficiently to support the clods with which they plaster this skeleton of a hut all over, except a small hole in the side for a window, a small door to creep in and out at, and a hole in the roof, stuck round with sticks, patched up with turf, for a vent, as they call a chimney. The covering of these huts is turf, cut about five or six inches thick, and put on as soon as taken from the moor; therefore it seldom loses its vegetation; as I hardly saw any difference between the huts and the moor; for what heath there was on either, was equally in bloom.

In these huts they make a fire upon the ground, and the smoke issues in columns at every hole, so that if an inhabitant within be induced to take a peep at any travellers, they are seen in a cloud of smoke; notwithstanding which, the curshes (caps of Highland women) were as white as snow, and the faces of the children mostly fair and blooming. At night they rake out the fire, and put the beds of heath and blankets (which they have in abundance) on the ground, where the fire had been, and thus keep themselves warm during the night.

The chief of their furniture is an iron pot, a few bowls, and spoons of wood, and pails to put their milk in.[17]

Alexander Carmichael, "Grazing and Agrestic Customs"

Alexander Carmichael (1832-1912) was a native of the island of Lismore who worked officially as a civil servant but spent decades collecting a wide variety of Gaelic folklore all over the Highlands. The following is extracted from a text written by Carmichael for the Report of the Crofter Royal Commission 1883-84 that was established to investigate the reasons for widespread political agitation in the Highlands, in response to Clearances and the abuses of landlords. Carmichael was conscious of his role as a mediator between Highland and Lowland Scotland at a time when anti-Gaelic prejudice was rife throughout Britain and Highlanders had virtually no political power to change the conditions that impoverished and disempowered them.

> The *maor* (native Gaelic constable) engages the herdsman and shepherd of the townland, apportions them ground for potatoes and bere, collects and pays their wages. These wages are self-levied on the crofters according to their rent, as they have a whole croft, a half croft, or a quarter croft.
>
> Every townland has a cattle fold on the *machair* ("grassy sands") and another on the *gearraidh* ("surrounding grazing pastures"). In wet weather the constable instructs the herdsman to keep the cows to the *machair*, where the fold, from the nature of the soil, is less wet and comfortless to the cows and the women who milk them, than the fold on the *gearraidh*.
>
> The constable must see that the dyke enclosing the cattle-fold is repaired in early summer before being used, and that the gate (*cadha-chliath na cuithe*, "the gate of the cattle-fold") is good and strong. The term *cadha-chliath* literally signifies the wattle gorge or pass.
>
> In wooded districts throughout the Highlands, where materials can be found, doors, gates, partitions, fences, barns, and even dwelling-houses, are made of wattle-work.
>
> In the case of dwelling-houses and their partitions, the wattling is plastered over on both sides with boulder clay, and whitewashed with lime, thereby giving an air of cleanliness and comfort to the house. ...
>
> The crofters say that the change from the low-lying plains to the bracing air of the hills was of benefit to themselves, and that as a consequence complaints common among them now were unknown. They talk with delight of the benefit derived in mind, body, and substance from their life among the hills. I entirely agree with them, and believe that these shrewd people are quite equal to their critics. ...
>
> The tenants of a townland will not willingly allow a fellow-tenant to sell his grazing outside the townland. There are various things which a tenant can do and which he cannot do; and all these things, so intricate to a stranger, so easy to themselves, are well defined.

All these stock and land arrangements of the people show that they could not have been devised in ignorance; nay, that the framers of these regulations must have been shrewd, intelligent people.

Should a tenant have an overstock of one species of animals and an understock of another species, these species are placed against one another. This is called *coilpeachadh*, which for want of a better term may be called 'equalising.' In like manner, if a tenant has an overstock of the old and an understock of the young of the same species of animals, the young and the old are placed the one against the other and equalised. After the *coilpeachadh* is done, should there still be a balance against the tenant, he must provide for it specially. This is done by buying grass from a neighbour who is short of stock, or from a tenant in a neighbouring townland. Or perhaps his fellow-tenants may allow the man to retain the extra cow, horse, heifer, stirk, or sheep, as the case may be, on the grass till he can dispose of it at the market. If so, they will exact payment for the grazing, and this payment is added to the general fund of the community towards purchasing fresh stock.

In these and all other matters the people are forbearing and considerate towards one another, and a man placed in any difficulty is aided to the utmost by his community. If, however, a man is obstinate, he is denounced as *fiacail gaibhre* "gaber tooth, goat tooth," standing out against the customs of the community. ...

Having finished their tillage, the people go early in June to the hill-grazing with their flocks. This is a busy day in the townland. The people are up and in commotion like bees about to swarm. The different families bring their herds together and drive them away. The sheep lead, the cattle go next, the younger preceding, and the horses follow. The men carry burdens of sticks, heather-ropes, spades, and other things needed to repair their summer huts (*sgitheil, bothain*). The women carry bedding, meal, dairy and cooking utensils. Round below their waists is a thick woollen cord or leathern strap (*crios-fhéile* "kilt-band"), underneath which their skirts are drawn up to enable them to walk easily over the moors. Barefooted, bareheaded, comely boys and girls, with gaunt sagacious dogs, flit hither and thither, keeping the herds together as best they can, and every now and then having a neck-and-neck race with some perverse animal trying to run away home.

There is much noise. Men – several at a time – give directions and scold. Women knit their stockings, sing their songs, talk and walk as free and erect as if there were no burdens on their backs nor on their hearts, nor sin nor sorrow in this world of ours, so far as they are concerned. Above this din rise the voices of the various animals being thus unwillingly driven from their homes. Sheep bleat for their lambs, lambs for their mothers; cows low for their calves, and calves low for their dams; mares neigh for their foals, and foals reply as they lightly trip round about, little thinking of coming work and hard fare. All who meet on the way bless the *triall*, as this removing is called. They wish the *triall* good luck and prosperity, and a good flitting day, and, having invoked the care of Israel's Shepherd on man and beast, they pass on.

When the grazing-ground has been reached and the burdens are laid down, the huts are repaired outwardly and inwardly, the fires are rekindled, and food is prepared. The people bring forward their stock, every man's stock separately, and, as they are being driven into the enclosure, the constable and another man at either side of the gateway see that only the proper souming has been brought to the grazing. This precaution over, the cattle are turned out to graze.[18]

Mary MacKellar, "The Sheiling"

Mary Kellar (*Màiri NicEallair*, 1834-90) was a native of Lochaber and a Gaelic poet. She wrote a number of valuable articles about Highland customs and work songs, including this description of how Gaels raised cattle and the foods they made from dairy products.

> Cattle were of so much importance to the Highlanders because they represented, in a special manner, their food supply. Milk, in its different forms, was their chief sustenance. Instead of the morning cups of tea, now indulged in by all classes of the community, they began the day by taking drinks of milk. Among the better classes, the morning drink (*deoch-maidne*) was what is known as "old man's milk," which was an egg switched into a glass of milk, with a little whisky added; and even the herd-boy got, if nothing better, a cup of whey to his piece of barley bread before turning out to tend the cows.

> When milk was scarce, the morning drink of the poorer people was *sùghan*, which is the juice of oatmeal or bran steeped so long as to become sour, and in very hard times they took it to their porridge. *Sùghan* was spoken of in song and story as a sign of poverty, as it indicated a scarcity of cows, and certainly it is not very palatable. ...

> The boys learned how to make and repair the milking and dairy utensils, to tend the flocks, shear the sheep, make and mend their own shoes; and to thatch, and make the heather and hair ropes so largely

used by them; and perhaps the most desired part of their education was the shooting of a blackcock, the stalking of a deer, and the spearing of a salmon.

The girls learned to emulate their mothers in skill of the dairy work, as well as in spinning wool for future webs on the distaff, and knitting stockings and hose of brilliant hues and rare patterns. They learned to know the herbs that were medicinal for man and beast, and the different plants used in dyeing the colours of their tartans. They learned to become useful wives, following in the footsteps of their mothers, as helpmates in the struggle for existence, neither fearing the snows and storms of winter, nor ashamed of the tawning of the summer sun. ...

A careful housewife was much more lavish with her butter and cheese to her household than she would be with either her warm milk or cream, as she took great pride in the quantities of dairy produce in her "cellar" at the end of the season. Yet there were times when even the richest cream would be freely produced, and this was especially at the demands of hospitality.

Water was never offered as a drink to the meanest wayfarer. *Deoch fhionna-ghlas* was the most effectual drink for quenching thirst. This "whitey-grey" mixture was milk and water in equal proportions, and the sour thick milk that was under the cream that was kept for butter was churned into a froth, and it made a cooling drink. It was called *sgathach*. When strangers had to be entertained, *fuarag* was made plentifully, and curds and cream were laid out with oatcake, butter, cheese and whisky.

They made the yearning, or yeast, that turned the milk into curds, by putting milk and salt into the stomach of a calf. The he-calves were generally killed, and their stomachs supplied them for this purpose. *Fuarag* was made of the sour thick cream, churned into a froth with a *lonaid* made for the purpose, and some oatmeal stirred into it. The meal made on the quern was considered by far the best for making it. This is a most delicious luxury, and a favourite with all classes. ...

The old life at the sheiling is a thing of the past. Yet, its traditions, and songs and proverbs that embalm its history, will live as long as our language is spoken or written, and the beautiful similes that tell of a pastoral people have become part of the mosaic that makes it so grand and worthy of preservation. Of a kind-hearted person it was said, *"Tha e mar am bainne blàth"* ("He is like the warm milk"). The poet could find no better thing to describe the fairness of the skin of his lady than to say she was as white as the curd. *"Cho geal 's an gruth leam fhéin thu."* "Calf-love" was described, *"laoigh na h-aon àirigh"* ("the calves of the same sheiling"). One going to marry a stranger away from their own people and glen was told in surprise, *"Ubh, ubh, b' fhada bho chéile crodh laoigh ur dà sheanar"* ("Ay, ay, the cattle of your two grandfathers would be far apart from each other"), and so on.

The boys brought up at the sheiling had a different stamina from the present generation who rejoice in being English-speaking and tea-drinking from their infancy. The new state of things fits them best for taking their places with the Lowlanders in the battle of life, but yet they unfit them to be the representatives of the race that grew up to be like a mighty bulwark to their country those who from childhood climbed the highest rocks, and swam the deepest pools, and whose simple, temperate lives fitted them for hardships and endurance.[19]

Anonymous, "The Dornoch Firth"

The following excerpts written by a member of Toronto Gaelic Society in the late nineteenth century recall memories dating back to the decades before the Potato Blight of the 1840s. They paint an idyllic picture of carefree youth growing up around the Dornoch Firth of Scotland and attest to a variety of wild foods available in the environment and knowledge of how to find and glean them.

Sgioladh, which we pronounced 'skeeloo', are shelled kiln-dried oats. All the people of the neighbourhood had their oats ground into meal there. We also got skeeloo, and all the carrots we could eat, for pulling Boyd's annual crop of carrots near the mill; and in the vicinity was Place Calltuinn, an extensive grove of hazel trees, where hundreds of bushels of nuts must have been annually gathered by the scholars and others; for by custom and usage the nuts were common property. It amazes me now to think of our capacities for *sgioladh*, and nuts, carrots, turnips, peas and beans, the buds of the fir, *mucaigean* (the wild-rose apples or hips), and lots of other raw stuff. …

On most of the farms of the district, individual fields were not separated from each other by fences; there were stone dykes along the roadways, but the margins and the divisions of the various fields consisted of brooks, wooded strips, and natural sod, along and amidst which the cattle found excellent pasturage; but they required to be herded to keep them from the growing and ripening crops, and all the young people on the farms, at one time or another had to take a turn at the "herding." But it was no work; it was just the grandest fun, the jolliest enjoyment of a succession of holidays in the finest weather of the year; we could, by turns, bathe in the firth; catch small trout under the stones in the burns; gather the various flowers, berries and roots in their season; swing on trees – the swings, with quite an extended stretch, constructed of the long, pliable and drooping branches of the white birch – we could search for birds' nests and wild honey; plait rushes into helmets; take flounders out of the *Cairidh*; make whistles of the alder and pipes of the oat-stalks; build small stone houses upon the shore; practice pole-jumping and putting the stone …

Blaeberries by the basketful were gathered in the hollows of the hills southwest of Ardgay, but they also grew in satisfactory quantities, and of extra good quality and size, all along the firth. Among the *grainnseag* vines and the heather, we, in the fall, got a great many nests of the red bee. The nest was a raised oval, about ten inches in diameter. With a stick we stripped off the roof, exposing the whole contents; the family was small, and the combs few – not much honey, but it was of a most exquisite quality and flavor.…

The whole district, in the valleys, is excellent for fruit-growing; all the small garden fruit and berries were good, also apples and pears, and I have seen apricots ripen well as wall-fruit.[20]

---

[1] Grant, *Highland Folk Ways*, 35-44.

[2] Ibid, 65, 71-75, 300-01.

[3] Ibid, 90-91, 94.

[4] Ibid, 160.

[5] Ibid, 65, 68, 71.

[6] Cheape, *Tartan*, 3, 7; Newton, *Warriors of the Word*, 195.

[7] Adapted from MacPhail, *Highland Papers*, vol. 1, 265.

[8] My translation of Watson, *Bardachd Albannach*, 148-57.

[9] Adapted from Munro, *Munro's Western Isles*, 42-43. Thanks to Hugh Cheape for pointing out the complexities of color in this passage.

[10] My translation from the transcription that appeared in *Gairm* 145 (1988-89), 65-66, with reference to Ó Baoill and Bateman, *Gàir nan Clàrsach*, 156-61.

[11] Hunter, *The Occult Laboratory*, 36.

[12] Campbell, *A Collection of Highland Rites*, 23, 25, 30; Hunter, *The Occult Laboratory*, 55-56, 58.

[13] Martin, *A Description of the Western Isles*, 22-23, 206-9, 291.

[14] Simmons, *Burt's Letters*, 84, 240.

[15] My translation from Campbell, *Òrain Ghàidhealach*, 154-62.

[16] Buchanan, *Travels in the Western Hebrides*, 6-7, 15-16, 84-85, 86, 87-88, 89, 93-94, 103-04, 115-16.

[17] Murray, *A Companion and Useful Guide*, 262-63.

[18] Carmichael, "Grazing and Agrestic Customs," 46, 145, 362-63, 364-65.

[19] Mackellar, "The Sheiling, I," 147-8, 152; "The Sheiling, II," 170.

[20] *The Scottish-Canadian* 22 January 1891; 12 February 1891; 19 March 1891.

Chapter Seven

From Birth to Death

Rites of Passage

This chapter will enable you to answer the questions:
• What are rites of passage and how do they bring structure and meaning to human life and social groups?
• What rites of passage were observed in the Scottish Highlands and what were the common elements in them?

Rituals and Meaning

Life is a constant process of growth, maturation, and revelation, from the joyous birth of a baby to the eventual certainty of death. Every indigenous culture recognizes different stages of life and has ways of marking the transition of the individual from one stage to the next, often by "rite of passage" ceremonies. The roles, obligations, and privileges a person enjoys is often determined by what stage of life they are in.

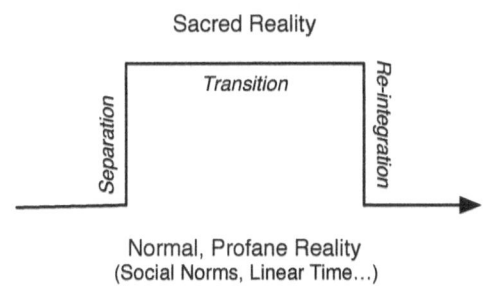

Diagram 7.1: *The structure of rites of passage*

Most rites of passage can be analyzed as consisting of three consecutive phases:
1. the separation of the individual from his or her previous environment and social role
2. the symbolic transition of the individual while in a state removed from mundane reality, normal social norms and the normal flow of time

3. the re-integration of the individual into the community, acknowledging his or her new state and the return to social norms

The period of transition between stages is typically considered to be a *liminal state* — a condition of being in-between — when normal restrictions and social constraints are relaxed. In Gaelic rites of passage, re-integration into the community typically includes the sharing of food and drink and the performance of song composed for the event.

The most important rites of passage in Highland society were those commemorating birth, baptism, marriage, and death. There was not a strict, unwavering script for any of these events, but they tended to include a common set of elements used in similar patterns across Gaelic Scotland and Ireland. While these were performed by people who had long been Christianized and considered themselves to be Christian, many of the beliefs and practices of these rites of passage reflect older cosmological traditions that were at odds with the strict interpretations of Christianity.

While secular Gaelic society remained resilient, the church was not able to remove traditional practices completely from the lives of its members. Many of the customs documented in the seventeenth and eighteenth centuries were the results of hybridization, as the church was increasingly able to impose its orthodoxies onto ancestral traditions. Tensions over the control of such rituals and their meaning were particularly pronounced at birth and at death.

Birth

The process of giving birth was dangerous for obvious reasons: childbirth is a common cause of death of women in non-industrial societies. The *bean-ghlùine* "mid-wife" was trained to assist with birthing and was usually a mother herself.

The immediate physical danger of childbirth was paralleled by anxieties about the spiritual well-being of the mother and child. Women in childbed and newly born infants were believed to be particularly vulnerable to being stolen by the fairies and replaced with changelings. They were under constant supervision and had special rites and charms administered to them for their protection. The advantage of this anxiety and supervision is that any medical complications that a woman or infant might have would be quickly noticed and attended to.

The child was not considered safe from Otherworld harm until he or she had been baptized, and the name was not said aloud until after it had been officially announced at the baptism.

The rituals surrounding birth typically included:
- Preparation: unlocking and untying everything
- Predictions about the child from day and hour of birth, other signs
- Separation
  - The child is born (separating him physically from his or her mother)
- Transition
  - First rites of welcome
  - Saining (providing magical protection to) mother and child

Baptism

The rites surrounding baptism commonly consisted of the following elements:
- Separation
  - Child is taken from home to church
    - Gift given to first person encountered
    - Omens read on journey (such as *ainm-rathaid* "road-name")
- Transition
  - Child baptized
  - Child given name
- Re-integration
  - Baptism feast
  - Omens read about child's future
  - Visitors and friends give silver to child

Marriage

In normal circumstances, a man and woman would have been courting and mutually ready for marriage. The *còrdadh* (also called the *réiteach beag*) were the occasions when the suitor informed his sweetheart or her father that he intended to approach her family for a full, formal betrothal, called the *réiteach (mór)*. In some cases, however, men went seeking brides they had never met, on the advice of others; such circumstances presented the possibility of failure during the negotiations of the *réiteach*. This ritual emphasized both the consent of the bride and her family to marry before public witnesses, and also fixed her *tochradh* "dowry."

The negotiations for the engagement were done on behalf of the suitor by the *gille-suiridhich* "courtship-helper, best-man," who would extol the virtues of his client eloquently and mediate the delicate arrangements between families so that the suitor himself could not be accused of being forward, overbearing, or acquisitive. The potential bride's family sometimes had their own spokesperson who fulfilled a similar function.

The successful conclusion of the *réiteach* moves the bride and groom into a liminal state between betrothal and marriage. As in many other cultures, the bride and groom were guarded and sometimes given ritual restrictions until the wedding occurred. After the betrothal was complete, but sometimes not until after the wedding itself, the couple began *faoighe* (called "thigging" in Lowland Scots): asking for donations of items that they needed to start a new household of their own.

The wedding was usually a large and joyous affair that included a great feast of food, music, and dancing. The mother of the bride greeted her the next morning and arranged her hair in the *bréid beannach* "pointed headkerchief," indicating her status as a married woman. After this ritual conferring of marital status some poet recited a blessing to her in verse, praising her beauty in the new headdress and giving her advice about marriage.

The full set of Gaelic marriage customs consisted of several stages, each successive stage becoming increasingly binding (in social and legal terms) and involving a wider segment of the community. Wedding practices typically consisted of the following elements:

- *Còrdadh / Réiteach Beag* "Initial proposal"
- Separation: *Réiteach (Mór)* "Betrothal"
  - Parties meet at sacred mound or bride's house
  - Verbal sparring and negotiations for dowry
  - (If groom's spokesman successful) Bride sits with groom, drink from same glass
  - Declaration of banns (in church or public place), make entry in registry book
  - Ritual blackening/cleansing of bride and groom
  - *Faoighe* "thigging" to gather initial assets for family
- Transition: *Banais(-taighe)* "Wedding ceremony"
  - Minister's blessing
  - Cake/bread broken over bride's head
  - Contention for good luck token (kiss, oatcake, stocking, etc.)
  - Marriage feast
    - Toast to couple
    - Poetic contributions or contests
  - Dance
    - Bride's maids take away bride secretly to bed chamber
    - Groom's friends take away groom
  - Bedding of couple

- Community puts couple into bed
- Ritual counteraction against spells
- Re-integration
  - Married women place marriage kerchief on bride's head
  - Bride is welcomed in verse

Death

Death and burial rituals in the Highlands tended to consist of the following elements:
- Portents of death seen or heard beforehand
- Last rites (if possible)
- Separation Part I
  - Death (i.e., soul is parted from body)
  - Clocks stopped, windows opened, mirrors covered or removed
- Transition
  - The body is prepared (closing eyes, washing, changing clothes)
  - Body is placed in coffin or bier
  - Wake
    - Body is watched especially at night
    - People pay respects to the deceased
    - Wake games, storytelling, keening, dance
- Separation Part II
  - Funeral procession from home to the burial site led by keening women, bagpipes or bell
- Re-integration
  - Body laid in the earth
  - Funeral feast

Primary Sources

Anonymous, *A Collection of Highland Rites and Customs*

This anonymous account, written in about 1685, provides brief details about customs performed at rites of passage. Many of these reflect on the role of gender in defining identity and social roles.

> When a male is born they put a sword or knife in his hand, and a spindle into the hand of a Female.

When they are carried out to be baptiz'd they cast a litle Fire after them; v.g. a litle coal, straw, &c.

Instead of Butter saps they mix meal & Ale together; which every person at the Feast must taste in order.

They put a piece of iron on the bottom of the Cradle, that no evil eye wrong the Child. ...

A lad born on Sunday they call Donald, a lass Jennet. ...

When they come from Church at their eating in the House they put the Child into a Basket full of Bread & Cheese, and then take him out, all who enter must (eat) thereof & then take a Drink. ...

The poorest are kept after death one night, & then they use disguises music of all kinds, Dancing all exercises of Agility. Every one who comes into the place where the corps is, prayeth over it.

In some places they had singing women who were called to Lac-wakes, & at Funerals where they diverted the Company. They called them from one parish to an other.

They generally desire to be buryed with their Ancestors.

The women make a crying while the corps is carried & when they have done, the Piper plays after the corps with his great pipe. When they come to the churchyard all the women (who always go along to the Burial place) make a hideous Lamentation together & then they have their particular Mournfull Song for their other Friends that lye there.[1]

Martin Martin, *A Description of the Western Isles*

Martin Martin provides us with many incidental details about Highland customs, including the role of chieftains in maintaining families and how people attempted to protect newly-born children from being stolen from the fairies.

When a Tenant's Wife in this or the adjacent Islands dies, he then addresses himself to Mackneil of Barray, representing his Loss, and at the same time desires that he would be pleas'd to recommend a Wife to him, without which he cannot manage his affairs, nor beget Followers to Mackneil, which would prove a publick Loss to him. Upon this Representation, Mackneil finds out a sutable Match for him; and the Woman's Name being told him, immediately he goes to her, carrying with him a Bottle of strong Waters for their Entertainment at Marriage, which is then consummated.

When a Tenant dies, the Widow addresseth herself to Mackneil in the same manner, who likewise provides her with a Husband, and they are marry'd without any further Courtship. ...

There is another way of the *Deiseil*, or carrying Fire round the Women before they are churched, after Child-bearing; and it is used likewise about Children until they be christen'd: both which are perform'd in the Morning and at Night. This is only practised now by some of the antient Midwives: I enquired their Reasons for this Custom, which I told them was altogether unlawful; this disoblig'd them mightly, insomuch that they would give me no satisfaction. But others, that were of a more agreeable Temper, told me the Fire-round was an effectual means to preserve both the Mother and the Infant from the power of evil Spirits, who are ready at such times to do mischief, and sometimes carry away the Infant; and when they get them once in their possession, return them poor meagre Skeletons: and these Infants are said to have voracious Appetites, constantly craving for Meat.[2]

Rev. John Buchanan, *Travels in the Western Hebrides*

It is not surprising that, as a missionary, some of Reverend John Lane Buchanan's observations on the customs he witnessed in the Outer Hebrides in the 1780s are peppered with judgmental comments. His notes demonstrate that Scottish Highlanders were not prudish people in the eighteenth century.

> The common, as well as the better sort of people, court sweet-hearts at nights, over all this country. The unlocked doors yield those lovers but too easy access to their favourites. The natural consequences of their encounters often occasion squabbles in kirk courts, in which minister and elders take cognizance of the fornication committed in the parish. ... The woman, if she is pregnant by a gentleman, is by no means looked down upon, but is provided in a husband with greater eclat than without forming such a connection. Instead of being despised, numberless instances can be produced, where pregnant women have been disputed for, and even fought for, by the different suitors. ...
>
> One would naturally wonder that women of easy virtue, as we before described, should not find it difficult to meet with helpmates; yet so it is, that many instances can be produced, when the men strive to get their favourite in spite of what may be alleged against her virtue.
>
> They make large weddings, and they frequently spend more money than their promised portion on the occasion; though they should want

in the after part of life. It is customary for both the bride and bridegroom, just before their marriage ceremony, to untie their shoes, garters, and some other bandage, to prevent witchcraft, of which they are much afraid on these occasions, and think this an antidote against it. …

Their baptisms are accompanied with ceremonies that are innocent and useful, for cementing the peace of the country, more especially among themselves. Baptism is administered either in public or in private; – just as it suits the conveniency of themselves and their minister. After this the parents present the child to some neighbour, and call him *goistidh*, or god-father; and after kissing and blessing the child, the *goistidh* delivers the infant to the mother, and ever afterwards looks upon himself as bound not only to be careful of that infant, but also very much attached to the parents. They call one another *goistidh*s during life. This name becomes more familiar to them than their own Christian names. …

Burials are preceded by the large bag-pipe, playing some mournful dirge. They continue playing till they arrive at the place of interment, while the women sing the praises of the dead, clasping the coffins in their arms, and lie on the graves of their departed friends …

On those occasions, there is great profusion of meat and drink brought to the place of interment, where the expenses generally bear a proportion to the rank and fortune of the person deceased, to prevent the imputation of meanness; and they seldom separate while the cask contains any spirits to wash down their sorrow: which seldom happens before their griefs are converted into squabbles, and broken heads, which some of them carry home as marks of remembrance for their lost friends.

They seldom display much mirth at late wakes, as they do in many parts of Scotland; but sit down with great composure, and rehearse the good qualities of their departed friend or neighbour. Their grief soon subsides after they are buried; and many have speedily replaced a lost wife by some of their former acquaintance.[3]

Sir Aeneas Mackintosh, "Notes Descriptive and Historical"

Sir Aeneas Mackintosh of Mackintosh wrote a fascinating account between the years 1774 and 1783 about the parish of Moy, south-east of Inverness, which draws on even older memories of customs, such as these rites of passage.

As soon as the partys have agreed upon the Day of Marriage the Clerk of the parish (sometimes the Parson) is sent for, and in the presence of their mutual Relations, a Writing called the Contract is signed, whereby the Parties bind themselves to marry, and in case of nonperformance (without just cause) to pay such a sum as is thought proper. The night before Marriage the Ceremony of feet washing is performed at the Bride and Bride Grooms own Lodgings; among the Men it is an excuse for drinking. Next morning, being dressed, the Bridegroom first (preceded by a Bag pipe,) having a young man on each side of him, next comes the Bride with her two Maids, proceed for Church; when the ceremony is over, and the partys come out, pistols and guns are fired over their heads by their acquaintances who then join, and a Cake broke over the Bride's head, when a great Struggle is made for a piece of it.

Upon their Return a Dinner is ready, Several Cows and Sheep being frequently killed for that purpose. When it is over the Bride Groom goes round the Guests with a plate, when every one gives according to his Inclination, and if the Bride and Bridegroom are liked, they get as much as will enable them to stock their farm. The Lord of the Manor frequently attends in order to encourage Matrimony ...

The Country people sometimes dance to a pipe, but oftener to the fiddle. At the commencement and finishing of each Reel or Dance the Swains kiss their Nymphs. The fiddler receives one penny for each Dance. The Highlanders have a sort of Dance performed by two people, bearing a great Resemblance to the Spanish Fandango. The Company continue dancing and drinking till the hour for the young peoples going to bed, when the whole accompany them to the Barn (for they are not allowed to sleep in the house the first night). All the men remain on the outside till the Bride is undressed, then, (the Bridegroom being undressed) they kiss the Bride, and after untying the latch of the left shoe which they imagine will take away the power from Witches, of preventing the Man from performing the marriage Rites (*ut vim coeundi ni fallor viris tollerent*) and also lock the Door, the key of which is deliver'd to the Bride's Mother.

Next morning it formerly was the Custom to ty a Basketfull of Stones round the Man's neck to show his Strength, for the cutting away of which the young Woman had a sharp knife. It was and is still a Custom to make the husband drunk the second night, that the Wife might know how to treat him on similar occasions. The wedding continues several

Days. If the young Couple are very poor, they frequently went round the country to Thigg, which is a gentle name for begging, when the farmers gave corn, and Shepherds sheep to stock the farm. The first work the married woman undertook was making her winding sheet, which put her in mind of mortality. ...

The Body is dressed and laid out, as in other Countrys; during the night all the deceaseds Relations and Acquaintances convene to watch the Body and this Ceremony is called Latewake; a good fire is put on (if in winter), plenty of whisky and snuff goes round, the young Folks play at several Country Games while the graver sort tell tales of Ghosts and Hobgoblens, every word of which they believe. As late as the year 1740, Music was introduced, and the nearest Relation began the Dance. It must have been really ridiculous, to see a Widow taken to dance, with tears in her Eyes. Also a piper preceded the Corps to the Grave, and frequently the Attendents got drunk after the interment.

The Body of the Dead is watched, but great decorum is observed. After the funeral an entertainment is given, and large Quantitys of Liquor drunk, the Expense of which often ruind the Children, therefore to prevent this barbarous Custom in Torn, all Burials must be in the forenoon.

If the person died in the Country the Entertainment is given before the Interment (if the Distance to the Church be great); if not, then the feast is given afterwards, when there are no bounds to the Drinking. Fifty years ago, at an Entertainment given before the funeral of a Lady Culloden, the Company got so drunk, that they reached the Burial place before they recollected that they had left the Corps behind. And in the year 1770 being present at the funeral of the Mother of the chief of the Clanvichgillevray aged 90, thirty dozen of Claret, besides other wines and Spiritous Liquors, were drunk.[4]

John Ramsay, *Scotsmen in the Eighteenth Century*

John Ramsay of Ochtertyre (1736-1814) was born near Blair Drummond in Stirlingshire, very near the border between Gaelic and Scots communities in the eighteenth century. Although he trained as a lawyer at the University of Edinburgh, he returned to his family's estate and soon thereafter took to researching the antiquities of Scotland, including that of the Highlands. He relied upon the expertise of Rev. James Stuart of Killin and his son, Rev. John Stuart of Luss, for details about the customs of the Highlands.[5]

Thus it was a received notion that a lying-in woman (newly-given birth) should never be left alone, for fear the fairies should steal her away, and substitute something in her room. Yet this notion, though seemingly ridiculous, was in the main sensible, since it secured her against the giddiness or neglect of her attendants. Before the Highlanders were disarmed it was common to have a broadsword half drawn at the head of the bed or below the bolster. And on the north-east coast it is the first business of a mid-wife to set a lighted candle at each corner of the bed; whilst in other (parts of Scotland) she takes a light or fiery peat and draws a circle thrice round the lying-in woman, moving it *deiseil* – i.e., according to the course of the sun. This rite was not, however, peculiar to this occasion, being used by the Highlanders in many of their superstitions.

In some districts, so soon as the child is born the midwife ties a straw round its middle and then cuts it in three pieces. A live coal, or some sparks of fire, are commonly thrown into the water in which the infant is first bathed; and in Skye they throw a little of the water into the fire. It is usual in Breadalbane to put the end of a new-cut ash stick into the fire, and to receive with a spoon the juice which then gushes out at the other end, a little of which is the first liquor put into the mouth of the new-born infant. It is uncertain whether this was done medicinally or with a superstitious view. ...

But there is hardly any country where parental authority is more passive than there. People marry very early, and without much regard to circumstances and hence their union is generally the effect of mutual liking ... Nor have parents the same reasons for crossing their children's affections as in countries where there is a greater inequality of circumstances ... It is, however, reckoned dutiful to consult them before entering into that state, because they may thereby expect their blessing, and a share of the little they have. ...

At the celebration of marriage there was a custom in some parts of the Highlands of leaving the latchet of the bridegroom's left shoe loose, and of putting a piece of silver under his heel. The purpose of it was to prevent the effect of charms and incantations. ...

No sooner did a person die than those about him lifted the body from the bed. And after being stretched, it was laid at full length on a board or plank of wood, set either on stools or two timber pins placed on the side of the wall; and above it, at some distance, another board was suspended from the roof, over which a plaid or other piece of cloth was thrown, which hung down like a canopy. When it became dark, candles or lights were set on the upper board. And it was also the custom to lay some iron, cheese, a plate with salt, and sometimes a green turf, on the dead person's breast. Some of these things were perhaps used to prevent the corpse from swelling; but the salt, the iron, and the cheese, intimate some purpose of superstition. ...

Between this period and that of interment, the friends and neighbours of the deceased assembled at night in the chamber where the corpse was laid. This was called *Faire-mhairbh*, or the late wake. The manner in which the Highlanders formerly behaved on these occasions must appear to strangers indecent and unnatural. During this period, nothing went on in the house of mourning but dancing and other amusements. ...

Upon the day of the burial, both men and women attended in great numbers. In old times it was the practice in the West Highlands (as it is still in Ireland) to hire women as mourners at the funerals of people of distinction. The females who were invited commonly sat in a cluster by themselves upon a neighbouring eminence till the corpse was brought out and laid upon two stools at the door. As soon as it appeared the women flocked around it, clapping their hands and raising hideous cries. And many of them tore their hair or head-dress, and shed tears plentifully.

The corpse was then put on a bier and carried successively by four men on their shoulders; the rest followed – a piper, or perhaps a number of pipers – playing some melancholy tune all the way before them. The chieftain's march was commonly the first played after they set out, and the last was one peculiarly plaintive ...

The women kept behind the men, bewailing at intervals, in broken extempore verses, the dead man; and praising him for his birth, his achievements in war, his activity as a sportsman, and for his generous hospitality and compassion to the distressed. This was called the coronach — i.e., the dirge. The women of each valley through which they passed joined in the procession, but they attended but a part of the way, and then returned. Even female passengers who accidentally met the funeral joined in the coronach, though perhaps strangers to the deceased. ...

As soon as the burial people approached the place of interment, two men were despatched before to mark out the grave. And when the corpse arrived, it was carried *deiseil* – i.e., according to the course of the sun – around the spot which had been chosen. After this ceremony, the body was laid down hard by; the pipers then gave over, the grave was dug, and the tartan plaid or other covering taken off. When the body was put into the earth, the women raised the coronach for a few minutes louder than ever, and then were silent. And after the grave was closed, the whole company sat down in the churchyard, and every person was served with meat, and liquor out of shells.[6]

Anne Grant, *Letters*

Anne Grant of Laggan relayed the following anecdote to illustrate the close bonds between different social classes, and the self-confidence and aplomb of the lower orders in their relations with the upper ranks. This story provides an interesting counter-point to the anecdote from Martin Martin near the beginning of this section: instead of the chieftain of the MacNeills of Barra providing a wife for a dependent in an autocratic manner, as might be assumed from Martin's account, in this anecdote one of the chieftain's servants expects to provide him with guidance on the same matter.

> There was in the family of Barra a great dearth of hereditary counsellors, yet every islander was ready in his own humble, or rather familiar, way to proffer advice.
>
> About twenty years ago (MacNeill of) Barra, without asking the consent of his islanders, came to Lochaber to solicit the hand of the beautiful and amiable daughter of Cameron of Fassfern, nephew to the banish'd Lochiel. Among the rowers that brought his boat from Barra was an old man of the lower class, who had been perhaps his father's foster-brother or one of the island sages.
>
> A few days after his arrival he was walking with other gentlemen in the street of Maryburgh (now Fort William) when old Ronald call'd out in his native tongue, 'Rory, do you hear? I say, Rory.'
>
> 'Yes, I hear you very well, but am engaged at present.'
>
> 'But wait, Rory, is it indeed true what I hear of your marriage?'
>
> 'Be quiet, I have gentlemen with me; I will speak with you again.'
>
> 'Nay, but Rory, dear Rory, be cautious, 'tis the mother of your children you are seeking; you do not need money; but is she prudent and modest, tell me that, Rory?'

And all this in a loud voice in the open street. I should have premised that Barra is a well-bred, respectable, worthy man, whose appearance and manners might claim distinction wherever he is seen. The man's freedom was not the grossness of vulgar familiarity, nor Barra's forbearance the want of dignity. It was the earnestness of affectionate simplicity on the one side, and the condescension of true greatness of mind on the other. There is a volume of character in this simple anecdote.[7]

William Stewart, *The Popular Superstitions*

William Grant Stewart was born in about the year 1799 in Highland Banffshire.[8] He published a book in 1821 that contains one of the earliest efforts to create a systematic account of folk beliefs and folk customs in the Highlands. It includes these colorful descriptions of the rituals of marriage and death. It is clear that from his remarks that the church, newly empowered in the Highlands, was successfully modifying the wake into a much more sober and constrained custom than it had been in previous generations.

> When a couple of young lovers propose to get married, the nearest relations of both parties meet to take the case into consideration; and, in general, it is no difficult matter for the lovers and their advocates to get a decision consonant to their inclinations. This is called the booking (*leabhrachd*) or contract, which is very often ratified by no other covenant than a few bottles of whisky. If the parties come to an understanding, the lovers are immediately declared bride and bridegroom; and some Tuesday or Thursday in the growth of the moon is fixed upon for the celebration of the nuptials.
>
> Meanwhile, to sustain the dignity of the bridal pair, from motives of policy as well as of state, they select from their kinsmen two trustworthy persons each, who are delegated to the other the male to protect the party from being stolen, (a practice once common, and not yet extinct,) and the female to act as maid of honour and lady of the bedchamber on the bridal occasion.
>
> A few days prior to the bridal day, the parties, with their attendants, perambulate the country, inviting the guests, on which occasion they meet with marked attention from old and young. The invitations are all delivered to the parties *propia persona* at their firesides; and if the wedding is to be a cheap one, a small present is sometimes offered to the bride, and accepted of. ...

Marching to the sound of the inspiring bagpipes, and the discharge of fire-arms, the bride's party proceed to the place appointed for the marriage. The bridegroom's party follow at some little distance; and both arrived at the appointed place of rendezvous, the bridegroom's party stand in the rear till the bride's party enter the meeting-house, agreeably to the rules of precedence, which on this occasion are decidedly in favour of the bride in all the proceedings of the day. ...

On the floor the dancers are beyond compare. Fired with emulation who shall win the dance, every nerve and muscle is put in active exercise. The lads are gaining greater agility every successive reel ... This scene lasts for some hours, until the presence of day warns the bride to prepare for the bedding. Wishing, if possible, to elude the public gaze, she attempts to steal away privately, when, observed by some vigilant eye, her departure is announced, and all push to the bridal chamber.

The door is instantly forced open, and the devoted bride, divested of all her braws, and stripped nearly to the state of nature, is placed in bed in presence of the whole company. Her left stocking is then flung, and falls upon some individual, whose turn to the hymeneal altar will be the next. The bridegroom, next led in, is as rapidly demolished, and cosily stowed alongside of his darling. A bottle and glass being then handed to the bridegroom, he rewards the friendliness of those who come forward to offer their congratulations, with a flowing bumper. When the numerous levee have severally paid their court, they retire, and leave the young couple to repose. ...

On the last offices of friendship being performed, the body is laid on a bed in that apartment of the house most commodious and suitable for the company; and the neighbours immediately collect in bands, to watch over the remains of departed friendship. During the silent hours of midnight, the solemnity of the occasion is heightened by the sound of sacred praise, and reading of the blessed Gospel. Such are now the laudable employments which have assumed the place of that revelry which formerly disgraced the Highland wakes, when immoderate drinking, dancing, wanton levity, and profane amusements, were the prominent features of such an assembly. It is true, the moderate use of liquor and singing of songs are still tolerated, but excess on these occasions is now unknown.

On the departure of every group, one of the friends in attendance conducts them to the melancholy bier, when each generally testifies the ardour of his friendship by shaking the hand, which now cannot feel his proffered kindness, and retires full of those solemn reflections which the scene is calculated to produce.

On the third day after the defunct's decease, if the person occupied no station above the ordinary level, the body will be led to its destined abode. This sorrowful day is early distinguished by melancholy arrangements. Verbal warnings having been previously circulated to the male inhabitants of the district, large and timeous preparations are necessary for their accommodation and entertainment. ...

When the weeping relatives have severally bade the corpse the last adieu, by imparting the farewell kiss to the cold and pallid lip of death, (which, nevertheless, is perhaps the sweetest we ever impart,) the dearest form is for ever concealed from their view.[9]

David Stewart, *Sketches of the Highlanders of Scotland*

David Stewart (1772-1829) was born at Garth Castle in Highland Perthshire when it was still strongly Gaelic-speaking. He was an officer in the Black Watch and became instrumental in the popularization of the image of the Highlander soldier as romantic figure. His book presenting Highland history and traditions in a highly militarized light established him as a suitable expert to help Walter Scott and others organize the Scottish pageantry that welcomed King George IV on his visit to Edinburgh in 1822.[10]

> The weddings were the delight of all ages. Persons from ten years of age to four score attended them. Some weeks previous to the marriage-day, the bride and bridegroom went round their respective friends, to the distance of many miles, for the purpose of inviting them to the wedding.
>
> To repay this courtesy, the matrons of the invited families returned the visit within a few days, always well supplied with presents of beef, hams, butter, cheese, spirits, malt, and whatever they thought necessary for the ensuing feast. These, with what the guests paid for their entertainment, and the gifts presented the day after the marriage, were often so considerable, as to contribute much to the future settlement of the young couple.
>
> On the wedding-morning, the bridegroom, escorted by a party of friends, and preceded by pipers, commenced a round of morning coifs, to remind their invited friends of their engagements. This circuit

sometimes occupied several hours, and as many joined the party, it might perhaps be increased to some hundreds, when they returned to the bridegroom's house. The bride went a similar round among her friends, each having their separate parties. The bridegroom gave a dinner to his friends, and the bride to hers. During the whole day, the fiddlers and pipers were in constant employment. The fiddlers played to the dancers in the house, and the pipers to those in the field. The ceremony was generally performed after dinner.

Sometimes the clergyman attended, sometimes they waited on him: the latter was preferred, as the walk to his house with such a numerous attendance added to the eclat of the day. On these occasions the young men supplied themselves with guns and pistols, with which they kept up a constant firing. This was answered from every hamlet as they passed along, so that, with streamers flying, pipers playing the constant firing from all sides, and the shouts of the young men, the whole had the appearance of a military array passing, with all the noise of warfare, through a hostile country.

The young couple never met on the wedding-day till they came before the clergyman, when the marriage rites were performed, with a number of ceremonies too minute to particularize. One of these was to untie all the strings and bindings on the person of the bridegroom; nothing to be bound on that occasion, but the one indissoluble knot, which death only can dissolve.[11]

Lilias Campbell, *Records of Argyll*

This description of a Highland funeral and wake, featuring the famous Highland character Rob Roy, is extracted from a traditional tale about the Campbells of Ardslignish, recorded from Mrs Lilias Campbell of Lochnell in the mid-nineteenth century.

At the funeral of this Ardslignish's father (in 1714) there were 4,000 men, under arms, attending the various chieftains; and before the mourners left the house, Rob Roy, who claimed kindred with the family, stepped up to the bier, declaring that, if he was not allowed to have the first lift of Lochnell's body, it would not be the only one that would leave the house. This demand was granted, undoubtedly rather because brawling was considered out of place at such a time than that so great a number of men would be intimidated even by Rob Roy.

On one occasion, when John Campbell of Ardslignish was going to leave home, he went to the kiln where it was customary for the dead to be taken between the time of decease and of interment; and while there, while speaking to the smith of the place, who was supposed to be gifted with second-sight, he was surprised to see the man's face suddenly change, and his gaze become riveted on one corner.

The smith, on being asked the cause of his extraordinary manner, said that he saw either Ardslignish or himself lying dead in the kiln, as the body was covered by a plaid woven in an unusual manner, and of which only two had been made one being in his possession, and the other in that of Ardslignish. To calm the man's agitation, the latter said that he would make it impossible that this dream should come to pass, as he would leave orders that, in the event of the smith's death, his body should not be taken to the kiln, and in his own case such a thing was obviously impossible; thus the dream could have no fulfilment. However, he forgot all about the circumstance, and left without giving the promised order, to find, on his return, that the smith was dead, and his body lying in the kiln, wrapped in the plaid, as he had predicted.[12]

Dugald MacDougall, *Records of Argyll*

The follow description of games played at wakes is extracted from a traditional tale about the MacLachlans of Kilbride, recorded in the mid-nineteenth century from Dugald MacDougall of Soraba.

One of the MacLachlans of Kilbride went to Glencoe to buy cattle. He happened to put up for the night at a house in which a dead body was lying. According to the custom of the Highlands a number of the young men of the glen were assembled to "watch it": in other words, there was a wake in the house.

The guests were plentifully supplied with whisky, and the spirit of revelry had scope and play among them. When the night was well advanced, games were started. MacLachlan took note of all that was said and done, and said to himself, "It would be better to be tonight where I was last night. My good sense forsook me when I came to this house."

He knew by the ways of the MacDonalds that they wished to pick a quarrel with him. One of their games was this: A man laid himself on his back on the floor, and he was to be lifted by the ankles. Several of the young men tried to perform the feat. Some of them could not move him at all, others could barely move him.

When MacLachlan's turn came, he lifted him off the floor and flung him over the partition among the cattle in the other end of the house. Immediately upon this he made for the door, and ran off as fast as he could, with the MacDonalds in full chase after him.[13]

William MacKenzie, *Book of Arran*

This account collected in the nineteenth century from the island of Arran depicts some of the mirth and merriment around betrothal customs.

It was common, if any one wanted to be introduced to a lass that he had taken a notion of, to take a mutual friend with him to act as 'go between.' And this mutual friend was termed the 'blackfoot.' It sometimes happened in the case of a backward wooer that the blackfoot himself found his way to the heart of the fair one, and then the 'blackfoot' was said to have turned out to be the 'whitefoot.'

When a girl got engaged to be married, the news spread quickly around among neighbours and friends, and they used to gather to the girl's house in the evenings, lads and lasses from all the houses round about, and help to tease the wool for her blankets. This wool was afterwards sent to the carding-mill to be carded and made into 'rowans,' and the rowans were spun into thread by the girl and her friends, which thread was sent off to the weaver and woven into blankets. This was quite a common custom in my boyhood, and may be still.

There is one custom to which I think it is worth while to draw attention, namely 'booking.' Before a marriage could take place a meeting was arranged between the parties to the contract and their friends. I do not know whether any of the elders or the minister were there, or whether there was signing of books.

But the custom to which I wish to call attention was this: After the party was assembled the bride-elect say, or the bridegroom-elect, waited and had ever so many of the company taken in to their, his or her, presence as would-be suitors. Some one, generally a wit of some sort – the 'blackfoot' – was chosen to present the suitors, and if it was the lad who was waiting he would bring in the lasses and married wives too – it didn't matter. The introducer would say something like, 'Here's a nice young lass now, will you take her for your wife ?'

'No,' the lad would say, 'I'll not have her, because' then he gave his reason: she was too fat or too lean, too tall or too short, she had a squint, etc., etc., or any fault he could think of. The fun was carried on with great good humour and the best of spirits; roars of laughter greeting the quaint remarks of the one chosen to do the introducing, or the awkward excuses which the hard plied and embarrassed youth would sometimes give as a reason why he would not marry each one till the real one was taken before him. This one, he would say, had all the good looks he would like to see his wife possessed of, and so he would marry her.

The same was gone through then with regard to the girl, and of course the greatest scope was given for the exercise of the humour of the introducer, who with less feeling or less fear of hurting the feelings of the lads, ran over all their recommendations, mostly invented for the occasion. Each would be refused in turn till the right lad was brought in at last.[14]

[1] Campbell, *A Collection of Highland Rites*, 77, 85, 86; Hunter, *The Occult Laboratory*, 69, 71.

[2] Martin, *A Description of the Western Isles*, 97, 117-18.

[3] Buchanan, *Travels in the Western Isles*, 109, 167-170.

[4] Mackintosh, *Notes Descriptive*, 33-36.

[5] Stiùbhart, "Keening in the Scottish Gàidhealtachd," 12.

[6] Allardyce, *Scotland and Scotsmen*, vol. 2, 420, 422-23, 427-31.

[7] Grant, "Mrs. Grant's Letters," 301-02.

[8] Gibson, *Gaelic Cape Breton Step-Dancing*, 192-93.

[9] Stewart, *The Popular Superstitions*, 187, 189, 192, 196, 197, 201.

[10] See Clyde, *From Rebel To Hero*, 128-29.

[11] Stewart, *Sketches of the Character*, vol. 2, xxii-xxiii.

[12] Campbell, *Records of Argyll*, 121.

[13] Adapted from ibid, 183.

[14] MacKenzie, *Book of Arran*, vol. 2, 309-10.

Appendix A
Writing A Research Paper

Understanding Thesis Statements

Many courses require that you write a research paper which often centers around a thesis statement. If you must complete an assignment of this type, it is crucial that you understand what a thesis statement is:
- It is a specific claim that can be argued and thereby shown to be true or false.
- It provides a specific goal and focus to the research paper.
- It says something of significance about the subject.
- It provides a road map, helping the reader anticipate the flow of the paper.

You can only expect to arrive at your final thesis statement after a lengthy process of reading evidence and thinking through the implications: formulating a thesis statement is not the first thing you do after choosing your topic. Before you develop an argument on any topic, you have to collect and organize evidence, look for possible relationships between known facts (such as surprising contrasts or similarities), and think about the significance of these relationships. Once you do this thinking, you will probably have a "working thesis," a guiding principle, an argument that you think you can support with evidence but that may need to be adjusted along the way.

The most common mistake students make is thinking that a statement of intent (such as "In this paper I'll be looking at...") is a thesis statement; it is not. A thesis statement looks more like "In this paper I'll prove that..."

Good and Poor Examples of Thesis Statements

- "The MacLeans have always been a proud clan." Poor: this is a weak and subjective claim. How can "pride" be measured? This is not a specific enough statement to prove or disprove.
- "Scotland has benefited greatly from the ingenuity and industriousness of the Campbells." Poor: this is too vague. A thesis statement is a specific claim that can be argued from some particular perspective or set of evidence.

- "In this paper, I'll examine the reasons why fosterage was a common practice in the Highlands." Poor: this is just a statement of intent, not a claim that can be proven true or false.
- "Although only thirty-eight people were killed in the Massacre of Glencoe, several Gaelic sources reflect confirm that the event became notorious amongst Highlanders because of its breach of Gaelic social norms." Good: this is specific and focused, and can be proven by examining surviving documentary evidence.

Are These Thesis Statements? Why or Why Not?

1. The MacDonalds of Glencoe have been around a long time.
2. In this paper, I will be examining the poetry of the Campbells.
3. Poetry composed for the Campbells claims Gaelic, Norman, and Brythonic ancestry for them.
4. I will be comparing poetry composed for the MacDonalds with poetry composed for the Campbells.
5. The origin story of the MacLeans reflects the consciousness of pan-Gaelic identities.

Thesis Statement Checklist

1. Have you stated your thesis statement clearly near the end of your introduction?
2. Does your thesis express a specific argument about your topic that can be proven true or false?
3. Does your thesis preview the structure of your argument?
4. Does your thesis offer your reader a new and interesting idea, one involving conflict or tension, revealing a problem, or setting up a framework for comparison or contrast?
5. Have you kept to approved course topics?

Research Process and Outline

If you are writing a research paper about the history or social customs of Scottish Highland clans, you must make an argument, convincing your reader of some claim by bringing together appropriate supporting evidence and following a logical line of reasoning. Following these steps may help to guide you in that process.

1. Choose an allowable topic.

2. Search thoroughly for sources (primary and secondary) related to it.
3. Read through these sources, taking notes:
    a. How can you apply the tools and techniques from your course to these texts?
    b. How do sources (especially secondary) agree or disagree with one another?
    c. How do different primary texts relate to each other?
    d. Can you infer personalities or agendas in these texts?
    e. How does the "internal" representation of Highland life contrast with the stereotypes created in English and Lowland sources?
4. Create an outline for your paper which sets forth a logical progression of ideas and evidence to support your argument:
    a. Decide what evidence to use and in what order.
    b. How does each piece of evidence support your thesis statement? Make it a link in the chain of logic.
5. Identify a thesis statement in the material you have read:
    a. Is there a pattern in the evidence that can be summed up?
    b. Is there a concept or process that is illustrated by the evidence?
    c. Is there a "story" that can be told with the evidence?
    d. Is there a question about people, events, and developments that has not been answered by the secondary sources?
6. Write the body of the paper by fleshing out the outline:
    a. Contextualize and analyze each piece of evidence carefully.
    b. Cite secondary sources to support your analysis.
    c. Create footnotes and citations for all sources, information, definitions, and ideas that are not your own.
    d. Anticipate what counter-arguments and alternative interpretations could be made: is there some way to either strengthen your argument in the face of these, or hedge your argument to provide for other possibilities?
    e. Having written the bulk of your paper, do you need to revise your thesis statement?
7. Write an introduction (about two paragraphs):
    a. What might a general reader not already know about the time, place, people, or other circumstances?
    b. Explain this background, especially as relating to your topic and thesis statement.
    c. Provide a "road map": what will you be discussing, what evidence will you use, etc.
    d. Conclude your introduction with your thesis statement.

8. Write your conclusion:
    a. Restate your initial thesis statement in a slightly different way.
    b. Demonstrate that it has been proven by the revisiting the evidence you have used (in summary form) and your analysis of that evidence.
    c. Make note (if appropriate) of how your analysis shows the difference between stereotypes and Gaelic history as lived and perceived by Gaels themselves.
    d. Make note (if appropriate) of how people in the past have made creative and selective use of their own past and tradition.
9. Ensure that your paper has all proper parts (title, bibliography, citations, etc.).

Bibliography

Allardyce, Alexander, ed. *Scotland and Scotsmen in the Eighteenth Century*, 2 vols. Edinburgh and London: W. Blackwood and Sons, 1888.

Bannerman, John. "The Scots Language and the Kin-based Society." In *Gaelic and Scots in Harmony*, edited by Derick Thomson, 1-19. Glasgow: University of Glasgow, 1988.

Barrow, G. W. S. "The lost Gàidhealtachd of medieval Scotland." In *Gaelic and Scotland / Alba agus a' Ghàidhlig*, edited by William Gillies, 67-88. Edinburgh: Edinburgh University Press, 1989.

Black, George. *The Surnames of Scotland: Their Origin, Meaning, and History*. New York: New York Public Library & Readex Books, 1962.

Boardman, Steve. "The Campbells and charter lordship in medieval Argyll." in *The Exercise of Power in Medieval Scotland c. 1200 - 1500*, edited by Steve Boardman and Alasdair Ross, 95-117. Dublin: Four Courts Press, 2003.

— and Alasdair Ross, eds. *The Exercise of Power in Medieval Scotland c. 1200 - 1500*. Dublin: Four Courts Press, 2003.

Brown, Hume. *Early Travellers in Scotland*. Edinburgh: James Thin, 1978 [1891].

Buchanan, George. *The History of Scotland*. Glasgow: Blackie, Fullarton & Co., 1827.

Buchanan, John L. *Travels in the Western Hebrides from 1782 to 1790*. London, 1793.

Buchanan, William. *Account of the Family of Buchanan*. Glasgow, 1733.

Cameron, John. *Celtic Law*. London: William Hodge, 1937.

Campbell, Archibald, ed. *Records of Argyll: Legends, Traditions, and Recollections of Argyllshire Highlanders*. Edinburgh: William Blackwood and Sons, 1885.

Campbell, Herbert. "The Manuscript History of Craignish." In *Miscellany of the Scottish History Society*, vol. 4, 177-302. Edinburgh: Scottish History Society, 1926.

Campbell, John G. *Clan Traditions and Popular Tales of the West Highlands and Islands, Waifs and Strays of Celtic Tradition 5*. London: David Nutt, 1895.

Campbell, John L., ed. *A Collection of Highland Rites and Customes*. Cambridge: D. S. Brewer, 1975.

— ed. *Òrain Ghàidhealach mu Bhliadhna Theàrlaich / Highland Songs of the Forty-Five*. Scottish Gaelic Texts 15. Edinburgh: Scottish Gaelic Texts Society, 1984 [1933].

— *Canna: The Story of a Hebridean Island*, 3rd ed. Edinburgh: Canongate, 1994.

Cameron, Alexander, ed. *Reliquiæ Celticæ*, 2 vols. Inverness: The Northern Counties Newspaper, 1894.

Cameron, John. *Celtic Law*. London: William Hodge, 1937.

Carmichael, Alexander. "Grazing and Agrestic Customs of the Outer Hebrides." *Celtic Review* 10 (1914-16): 40-54, 144-48, 254-62, 358-75.

Cheape, Hugh. *Tartan*. 2nd ed. Edinburgh: National Museums of Scotland, 1995.

Clancy, Thomas Owen. "Scotland, the 'Nennian' recension of the *Historia Brittonum*, and the *Lebor Bretnach*." In *Kings, Clerics and Chronicles in Scotland, 500–1297*, edited by Simon Taylor, 87-107. Dublin: Four Courts Press, 2000.

Clark, James Tochach, ed. *Genealogical Collections Concerning Families in Scotland, Made By Walter MacFarlane*, 2 vols. Edinburgh: Scottish History Society, 1900.

Clyde, Robert. *From Rebel To Hero*. East Linton: Tuckwell Press, 1995.

Coira, M. Pía. *By Poetic Authority: The Rhetoric of Panegyric in Gaelic Poetry of Scotland to c.1700*. Edinburgh: Dunedin Press, 2011.

Constable, Archibald, trans. *John Major's History of Greater Britain*. Edinburgh: Scottish History Society, 1892.

Dodgshon, Robert. *From Chiefs to Landlords*. Edinburgh: Edinburgh University Press, 1998.

– *The Age of the Clans: The Highlands from Somerled to the Clearances*. Edinburgh: Birlinn, 2002.

Foster, Sally. "The Topography of People's Lives: Geography until 1314." In *The Edinburgh History of Scottish Literature*, vol. 1., edited by Thomas Owen Clancy and Murray Pittock, 44-51. Edinburgh: Edinburgh University Press, 2007.

Gannon, Megan. "Ancient DNA Sheds New Light on the Biblical Philistines." *Smithsonian Magazine* website https://www.smithsonianmag.com/science-nature/ancient-dna-sheds-new-light-biblical-philistines-180972561/ Accessed July 14, 2019

Gibson, John. *Gaelic Cape Breton Step-Dancing*. Montreal: McGill-Queen's University Press, 2017.

Gillies, William. "Some aspects of Campbell history." *Transactions of the Gaelic Society of Inverness* 50 (1976-8): 256-95.

Grant, Anne. *Essays on the Superstitions of the Highlanders of Scotland*. London: Longman, Hurst, Rees, Orme and Brown, 1811.

— "Mrs. Grant's Letters." In *Wariston's Diary and Other Papers: Publications of the Scottish History Society vol. XXVI*, 251-350. Edinburgh: Scottish History Society, 1896.

Grant, I. F. *Highland Folk Ways*. London: Routledge, 1961.

Henderson, George. *Survivals in Belief among the Celts*. Glasgow: MacLehose and Sons, 1911.

Hunter, Michael. *The Occult Laboratory: Magic, Science and Second Sight in Late Seventeenth-Century Scotland*. Woodbridge: Boydell Press, 2001.

Lynch, Michael. *Scotland: A New History*. London: Pelico, 1991.

MacDonald, T. D. *Gaelic Proverbs and Proverbial Sayings*. Eneas MacKay: Stirling, 1926.

MacGregor, Martin. "Gaelic Barbarity and Scottish Identity in the Later Middle Ages." In *Mìorun Mòr nan Gall, 'The Great Ill-Will of the Lowlander'? Lowland Perceptions of the Highlands, Medieval and Modern*, edited by Dauvit Broun and Martin MacGregor, 7-48. Glasgow: University of Glasgow, 2007.

— "Writing the history of Gaelic Scotland: A provisional checklist of the 'Gaelic' genealogical histories." *Scottish Gaelic Studies* 24 (2008): 357-380.

MacKay, Æneas J. G., ed. *John Major's History of Greater Britain*. Edinburgh: Scottish History Society, 1892.

MacKellar, Mary. "The Sheiling: Its Traditions and Songs, I." *Transactions of the Gaelic Society of Inverness* 14 (1888), 135-53.

— "The Sheiling: Its Traditions and Songs, II." *Transactions of the Gaelic Society of Inverness* 15 (1890), 135-53.

MacKenzie, William. *The Book of Arran*, vol. 2. Hugh Hopkins, Glasgow: 1914.

Mackintosh, Aeneas. *Notes Descriptive and Historical principally relating to the Parish of Moy in Strathdearn*. Inverness: privately printed, 1892.

MacPhail, J. R. N., ed. *Highland* Papers, 3 vols. Edinburgh: Scottish History Society, 1914-1920.

MacPherson, John. *Critical Dissertations on the Origin, Antiquities, Language, Government, Manners and Religion of the Antient Caledonians, Their Posterity the Picts, and the British and Irish Scots*. Dublin: Boulter Grierson, 1768.

Martin, Martin. *A Description of the Western Islands of Scotland*. London, 1716.

Matheson, William. *Highland Surnames*. Inverness: An Comunn Gàidhealach, 1973.

McLeod, Wilson and Meg Bateman, eds. *Duanaire na Sracaire / Songbook of the Pillagers: Anthology of Scotland's Gaelic Verse to 1600*. Edinburgh: Birlinn Ltd, 2007.

Mitchell, Arthur. "Vacation Notes in Cromar, Burghead, and Strathspey." *Proceedings of the Society of Antiquaries of Scotland* 10 (1875): 603-89.

Munro, R. W., ed. *Monro's Western Isles of Scotland and Genealogies of the Clans, 1549*. Edinburgh: Oliver and Boyd, 1961.

— "The Clan System: Fact or Fiction?" In *The Highlands in the Middle Ages*, edited by Lorraine Maclean, 117-29. Inverness: Inverness Field Club, 1981.

Murray, Sarah. *A Companion and Useful Guide to the Beauties of Scotland*. London: 1799.

Newton, Michael. *Warriors of the Word: The World of the Scottish Highlanders*. Edinburgh: Birlinn, 2009.

Nicolson, Alexander, ed. *Gaelic Proverbs*. Edinburgh: Birlinn Ltd., 1996 [1881].

Ó Baoill, Colm and Meg Bateman, eds. *Gàir nan Clàrsach / The Harp's Cry: An Anthology of 17th-century Gaelic Poetry*. Edinburgh: Birlinn Ltd, 1994.

Ommer, Rosemary. "Primitive accumulation and the Scottish clann in the Old World and the New." *Journal of Historical Geography* 12 (1986): 121-41.

Patterson, Nerys. *Cattle Lords & Clansman*. 2nd ed. Notre Dame: University of Notre Dame Press, 1994.

Pennant, Thomas. *A Tour in Scotland and Voyage to the Hebrides, 1772*, ed. Andrew Simmons. Edinburgh: Birlinn, 1998 [1774-6].

Pilkington, Nathan. "Five myths about the decline and fall of Rome." *The Washington Post*, December 2, 2016.

Sellar, W. D. H. "Celtic Law and Scots Law: Survival and Integration." *Scottish Studies* 29 (1989): 1-27.

Simmons, Andrew, ed. *Burt's Letters from the North of Scotland*. Edinburgh: Birlinn, 1998 [1754].

Sinclair, Alexander MacLean. "The Macintyres of Glennoe." *Transactions of the Gaelic Society of Inverness* 18 (1891-92): 289-94.

Stewart, David. *Sketches of the Character, Manners, and Present State of the Highlanders of Scotland*, 2 vols. Edinburgh: Archibald Constable, 1822.

Stewart, William G. *The Popular Superstitions and Festive Amusements of the Highlanders of Scotland*, 2nd ed. Edinburgh: Oliver and Boyd, 1851.

Stiùbhart, Domhnall Uilleam. "Women and Gender in the Early Modern Western Gàidhealtachd." In *Women in Scotland c. 1100-c.1750*, edited by Elizabeth Ewan and Maureen Meikle, 233-50. East Linton: Tuckwell Press, 1999.

—— "Uses of Historical Traditions in Scottish Gaelic." In *Oral Literature and Performance Culture, Scottish Life and Society* 10, edited by John Beech, et al, 124-52. Edinburgh: John Donald, 2007.

—— "Keening in the Scottish Gàidhealtachd." In *Death in Scotland*, edited by Peter Jupp and Hilary Grainger, 127-46. Oxford: Peter Lang, 2019.

Van Hamel, A. G., ed. *Lebor Bretnach: The Irish Version of the Historia Brittonum ascribed by Nennius*. Dublin: Stationary Office, 1932.

Watson, William. *Bardachd Albannach: Scottish Verse from the Book of the Dean of Lismore*. Edinburgh: Scottish Gaelic Texts Society, 1937.

About the Author

Dr. Michael Newton earned a Ph.D. in Celtic Studies, with a focus on Scottish Gaelic Studies, from the University of Edinburgh. He is a fluent Scottish Gaelic speaker who has pioneered the study of materials from the margins of the Gaelic world, especially the North American diaspora.

He was recognized with the inaugural Saltire Award from the Scottish Heritage Center of St. Andrews University, Laurinburg, North Carolina, in 2014 for outstanding contributions to the preservation and interpretation of Scottish history and culture. In 2018 he received the International Award at the annual Gaelic Awards ceremony in Glasgow, Scotland, for contributions to the wider Gaelic community.

He has published a multitude of books and articles about Scottish Highland heritage, history, and culture in Scotland and the diaspora. The books that he has written or edited include:

with Wilson McLeod. *An Ubhal as Àirde / The Highest Apple: An Anthology of Scottish Gaelic Literature*. London: Francis Boutle Publishers, 2019.

Warriors of the Word: The World of the Scottish Highlanders. Edinburgh: Birlinn, 2019 (2nd ed.).

Seanchaidh na Coille / Memory-Keeper of the Forest: Anthology of Scottish Gaelic Literature of Canada. Sydney: Cape Breton University Press, 2015.

The Naughty Little Book of Gaelic. Sydney, Nova Scotia: Cape Breton University Press, 2014.

Celts in the Americas. Sydney: Cape Breton University Press, 2013.

Bho Chluaidh gu Calasraid / From the Clyde to Callander: Gaelic Tales, Songs and Traditions from the Lennox and Menteith. Glasgow: Grimsay Press, 2010 (2nd. ed.).

Dùthchas nan Gàidheal: Selected Essays of John MacInnes. Edinburgh: Birlinn, 2006.

with Rhiannon Giddens. *Calum and Catrìona's Welcome to the Highlands*. Chapel Hill: Saorsa Media, 2006.

"We're Indians Sure Enough": The Legacy of the Scottish Highlanders in the United States. Chapel Hill: Saorsa Media, 2001.

www.ingramcontent.com/pod-product-compliance
Lightning Source LLC
Chambersburg PA
CBHW030444300426
44112CB00009B/1148